made you look
made you th!nk
made you "talk"

First published in 2008 by Millgate House Publishers.

Millgate House Publishers is an imprint of
Millgate House Education Ltd
30 Mill Hill Lane
Sandbach
Cheshire CW11 4PN, UK

Edited by Brenda Keogh and Stuart Naylor.

Graphics, layout and CD ROM design by Millgate House Education Ltd.

Printed by Crewe Colour Printers Ltd.

British Library Cataloguing in Publication Data
A catalogue record for this book is available from the British Library.

ISBN 978-0-9556260-2-9

Acknowledgements

No book is ever shaped and written by a single hand.

Over the course of several years, this book has developed from its original concept, as a resource for teachers to encourage young children to observe, think and talk, into something even more valuable.

This development has been guided by Brenda Keogh and Stuart Naylor, whose constant support, enthusiastic input and positive editing has been an inspiration. Their own experiences while writing and producing a range of high quality educational texts, have provided them with the knowledge and understanding to give sound, practical advice on every aspect of publishing.

The photographs of children at work have been taken in several schools that I have visited. My warmest thanks go to all those Head Teachers, classroom practitioners and families, who allowed me to work with their children and provide exemplification of many of the ideas contained in 'Made You Look!'.

The children themselves have been delightful and very patient with the visiting 'science lady'. As I asked for explanations of their experiences, on more than one occasion a child's response reminded me of a passage from 'The Little Prince' by Antoine de Saint-Exupery: 'Grown-ups never understand anything for themselves and it is tiresome for children to be always and forever explaining things to them.'

The Association for Science Education, the largest subject association in the U.K., has been a source of information and help, and continues to support all of us involved in science education.

I must also offer my grateful thanks to the graphic designer, Mel Wood, for her creativity, attention to detail and constant good humour. Her considerable skills allow her to take a simple suggestion and turn the outcome into something engaging, helpful and entertaining. If you find the book appealing and amusing in design and layout, it is largely due to Melissa's efforts.

Finally, I must thank all of my family, and particularly my husband Peter, for their unstinting encouragement throughout the process of writing this book.

Schools

Aberbargoed Primary School, Bargoed, Caerphilly

Cwrt-henri Primary School, Carmarthenshire

Cwrt Rawlin Primary School, Caerphilly

Little Folk Playgroup, Llanilltud Faerdref, Pontypridd

Llanfaes Primary School, Brecon

St. Robert's Primary School, Bridgend

Talgarth Primary School, Talgarth, Powys

Ysgol Ifor Bach, Senghenydd, Caerphilly

Families

Richard, Becky, Olivia and Oscar James

David, Claire and Jessica Powell

Index

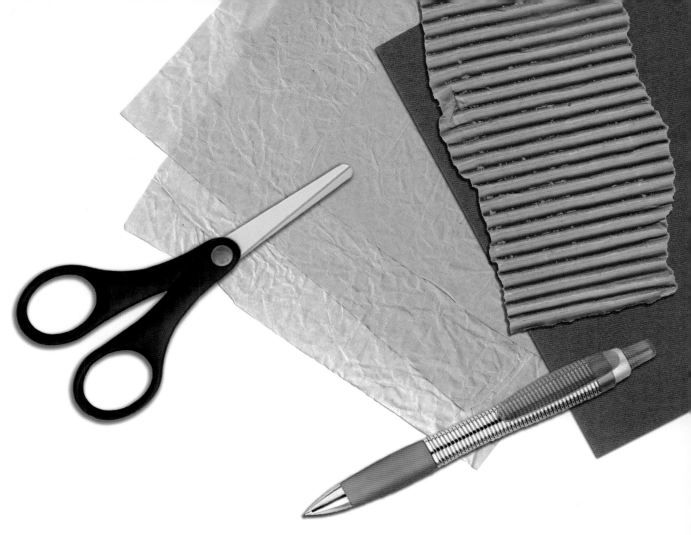

Introduction

Working with young children is an exhilarating experience. Young learners are typically enthusiastic, and interested in everything they see and do. Science is a wonderful subject for catching their attention and providing the 'wow' factor in the classroom. Even so, many teachers tell me that they feel insecure in their delivery of the science aspects of the curriculum. They are never too sure if they are 'doing it right'.

I am frequently asked to provide enjoyable activities for science that can be used immediately in the classroom. In many cases, when children take part in an activity it will be a brand new experience. Ideally, they will use all of their senses, develop good observational skills, and learn to communicate their experiences effectively.

With this in mind, the initial idea behind 'Made you look, Made you think, Made you talk' was to provide a series of simple, stimulating activities that would make children look, think and talk about what they had experienced.

During its writing, the publication has grown and developed into something more substantial than a collection of activities. Each chapter now includes:

● Guidelines for how to prepare and use the activity

This section includes key questions that you might ask.

● Looking for evidence of thinking and learning

Engaging the children in exploring science in a happy, supported lesson, and allowing them the space to think and discuss their understanding, will give you, and the children, plenty of opportunities to recognise, assess and celebrate their progress. To help you in this process, this section contains suggestions for what children might learn and experience, as well as the range of different opportunities the activity provides for their thinking and learning to be identified and developed.

● Illustrations of how the children have used the activity

● Ideas for extension activities based on Active Assessment strategies

These strategies help to challenge children's ideas and help to take their thinking further, so that the activities become more than simply good fun. They make thinking, learning and assessment an active and engaging process for children. Active Assessment strategies can also lead children into wanting to learn more about something, so that assessment and learning become integrated into one seamless process. For each activity, one of the suggested Active Assessment strategies is developed in some detail to show how it can be used. A worksheet is provided to exemplify the idea. Worksheets, and in some cases other resources, are on the CD so that they can be printed out.

Three further sources of support are also provided:

- An introduction to the Active Assessment strategies
- Guidelines for creating a supportive atmosphere to encourage children's talk
- References and details for suppliers of resources

The 'Looking for evidence of thinking and learning' section is based on a framework developed by Brenda Keogh and Stuart Naylor, first published in Bird and Saunders (2007). For more information about Active Assessment see Naylor, Keogh and Goldsworthy (2004). Active Assessment strategies used throughout the book are drawn from a range of sources, including DCELLS (2006).

Using Active Assessment strategies to promote talk, reveal understanding and advance learning

This section contains general information about the Active Assessment strategies used in the book. Active Assessment strategies are designed to create opportunities for children to talk about, and explore, their ideas. They can be used with individuals, but have a greater impact on learning where children are encouraged to talk with each other. Younger, or less confident, children may need some support or teacher mediation. In this way, children challenge each other's ideas and make explicit what they do, and do not, think and know. Children become active in the learning and assessment process, and begin to set their own agenda for learning.

Annotated drawing

Asking children to include words on their drawings allows them to communicate more detail about what they see or think. It also encourages them look more closely. Children may not be skilled enough to show a dimpled orange skin, but they can use words to express how the skin looks, feels and smells. Words can, of course, be scribed for pre-writers.

Asking for Annotated Drawings at the beginning and the end of a topic helps you, and the children, to see how much they have learned. An example can be seen in Activity 5, Drawing Partners.

Classifying and grouping

Classifying and grouping provide opportunities for children to discuss different possibilities, explain their ideas to each other and try to reach consensus. They learn how to observe carefully, look for patterns and make generalisations. While they do this, they provide evidence of their developing understanding.

We tend to use classifying and grouping interchangeably, though they are subtly different. When we classify, we usually use criteria to sort things; when we group, we usually put things into groups where the criteria are not fixed in advance. An example of Classifying and Grouping can be seen in Activity 1, Feely Walls.

Compare and contrast

Children are more likely to notice differences rather than similarities between objects. The compare and contrast approach encourages children to develop their observational skills and look for similarities as well. For example, a spider and a housefly could be compared and contrasted in terms of:

- how they move
- the shape of their body
- how many legs they have
- and so on.

Graphic organisers can be used to help children to compare and contrast. They challenge thinking as children try to reach agreement about their ideas, as well as providing direct evidence of their understanding. A Compare and Contrast example can be seen in Activity 26, Feet Family.

Concept Cartoon™

A Concept Cartoon uses a cartoon-style format, with different characters having different ideas about an everyday situation. For example, a group of children might be arguing about whether to put a coat on a snowman.

"Don't put the coat on the snowman. He'll melt."
"I think it will keep him cold and stop him melting."
"I don't think it will make any difference."

By showing a range of ideas, children are invited to join in the dialogue and explore what they think. They see that there are many possible ideas, so are encouraged to explain and justify what they think. This leads naturally to finding answers through investigation and research. An example of a Concept Cartoon can be seen in Activity 21, Summer Snow.

Concept map

Concept maps are generally used with older learners, but can be used with younger children. If children have limited writing skills, you can use pictures and arrows instead of words. Children will need to be shown how to use a concept map. Some children will then be able to generate ideas with only limited adult support.

Individual concepts are shown in boxes as pictures or words. Lines are drawn to link the concepts and linking words are added to these lines. Active words, such as eats and freeze, make the best linking words. Arrowheads show which way to read the links. Here's how you can help children to learn how to create a concept map:

- Write down, or collect from the children, the key words about a familiar topic. For example, if the topic is Living Things, the terms might include animals, dogs, plants, birds, or eggs.
- Write each word on a separate piece of paper or card, so that they can be moved around. Don't use too many words. Use pictures as well as words where you can.
- Ask children which words they think are connected and why. As you discuss the concepts, emphasise the links between them.
- The cards are arranged so that related terms are close to each other. For example, eggs are close to animals that lay them. These words are then linked with arrows.

- You can have some simple linking words already available on card arrows, or write words that children suggest on blank arrows.
- When everyone is happy, the cards can be stuck onto a large piece of paper or can be left for children to explore and discuss further on their own.

If you haven't seen a concept map before, you can see examples in Novak and Gowin (1984), White and Gunstone (1992), Naylor, Keogh and Goldsworthy (2004) or you can find plenty on the internet. You can see an example of Concept Mapping in Activity 18, Racing Liquids.

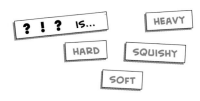

Concept sentences

Children are presented with the problem that they need to fix some broken sentences because you don't know how to put them together. You provide a number of key words on cards, with pictures where possible. Children use these words to form sentences. They can add words of their own on blank cards to help them complete the sentences. Each word can be used more than once.

Make sure that there are adjectives as well as nouns. Provide pictures to accompany the nouns whenever possible. Encourage children to talk about their sentence as they create it. To create their sentences, children may want to try something out or check their ideas. An example of Concept Sentences can be seen in Activity 25, Feely Feet.

Create a list of instructions

Here children are challenged to set out a series of instructions for someone else to follow. The children can generate the instructions themselves, or you can supply the individual steps on strips of card for them to arrange. By talking through the sequence, children may have their ideas challenged or may clarify their ideas by asking questions about the process.

This strategy is generally used towards the end of a topic, when children have absorbed enough information to apply their learning. For example, having made a jelly in class, the children could think about the individual actions needed to get it to the stage where you can eat it. An example of this strategy can be seen in Activity 7, Flitter Jars.

Create a story

Stories are exciting, enjoyable and fun. Setting a problem or series of facts in a story format can make it more real and help children engage more quickly. Through engaging in the story, children will share their ideas, consider possibilities, describe what is happening, and explain their thinking. For example, in Activity 25, Feely Feet; you might Create a Story along the lines of 'We're Going on a Bear Hunt' (Rosen and Oxenbury, 1993). An example of this strategy can be seen in Activity 6, Let Me Out!

Deliberate mistakes

As the name suggests, this approach relies on you showing or doing something which is incorrect, and the children spotting what's happened. Using deliberate mistakes helps children to clarify their own ideas by observation and discussion with others. It helps you to assess how they respond to the deliberate mistakes. Do they notice the mistakes, and how do they think the mistakes should be corrected? It's helpful to indicate that you might make a mistake, such as "I'm feeling a bit confused today, so I might not get everything right. Can you help me, and let me know if you spot me making any mistakes?"

For example, you might begin a sorting exercise by putting creatures with varying numbers of legs into different groups. If you put an insect in the 2-legged creatures group, the error should be spotted quite quickly, whereas a crab in the 6-legged creatures group might be missed. An example of Deliberate Mistakes can be seen in Activity 24, Paper Clip Spinners.

Hot seating

In this strategy, one child or a pair of children is selected to act as 'experts', or to assume the role of a character, such as a zookeeper. They can be given information or do some 'research' into their topic beforehand. The rest of the class can ask up to 10 questions to find information about a particular animal. Alternatively, the children have to guess which animal the experts have researched by asking pertinent questions. The expert only answers 'yes' or 'no'. For example:

- Does this animal live in water?
- Does it lay eggs?

Children soon learn which questions give the most information, and this can lead to useful discussion about how to find out information and which are the best kinds of questions to ask. An example of this strategy can be seen in Activity 5, Drawing Partners.

KWHL grid

These simple 4-column grids set out what learners **Know** about a topic, what they **Want** to know about it, **How** they think they will find out and then what they have **Learnt** by the end. In principle the grids can be used by individual children, but working together on the grid is more productive.

- You could discuss a topic, such as minibeasts, with the class to find out what they think they know.
- You can record the points that they make in the first column.
- Then the children can think about what they would like to know and how they would find out the answers.
- Finally, after research or enquiry, the last column can be completed to show what has been learned.

An example of a KWHL Grid can be seen in Activity 3, Spider.

Making a list

This is a simple strategy for children to use to share their ideas. It is a useful start to a topic when you want to check what the children already know. It generates ideas for further enquiry. As with many of these Active Assessment approaches, it is possible to do this with individuals. However, a group discussion is more useful, where sharing ideas acts as a catalyst for modifying, extending and learning new ideas.

For example, making a list of things that sink raises all sorts of questions, such as:

- whether all the children agree on what will sink
- whether you can do something to make an object float or sink
- how they might predict whether something will sink

During the discussion you can collect any words or ideas raised by the children, ideally on a whiteboard or flip chart. This could form part of a display that supports the children's work during that topic. An example of Making a List can be found in Activity 14, Find Me a Rainbow.

Moving from describing to explaining

The foundation of good science is the ability to make good observations, using all the senses. As children develop, they learn that their descriptions of observations can lead towards simple explanations. Explaining is a higher order skill, and involves greater thinking than simply describing what is in front of them. "You've said the sandpaper feels rough and the writing paper is smooth. What do you think makes the sandpaper feel so rough?"

Even when children can't articulate their thinking, it is useful to get them to think about explanations. By encouraging them to think about why something is happening, we help them to see the value of explanations. In order to explain clearly, children may want to do more exploration and therefore take their ideas further. An example of Moving from Describing to Explaining can be seen in Activity 1, Feely Walls.

O.P.O.E Observe, predict, observe, explain

In this strategy you ask the children to follow the sequence of:

- observing something
- predicting what they think will happen next
- observing what actually happens
- then trying to explain what happens.

With older children the sequence is normally predict, observe, explain (see White and Gunstone, 1992). However, with younger children, the initial observation helps to set the scene for thinking, as well as engaging the children. Younger children generally will not have enough information to make proper predictions. For them a prediction is most likely to be a judgement or an informed guess. Their predictions might be verbal, drawn or written. An example of O.P.O.E can be seen in Activity 13, Liquid Layers.

Odd one out

Odd one out is a very simple strategy which children love. Although it seems just like a game, it is a really valuable stimulus for reasoning, classifying, understanding properties, learning key vocabulary, and so on.

You can do this by using a short list or showing a set of pictures. For example, "Duck, seagull, frog, sparrow . . . Which is the odd one out? Think about where they live, how they move, what their legs are like, and so on." If there is more than one possible answer, as there usually is, this can lead to mature class discussion and helps develop the higher order skill of explanation. An example of the Odd One Out strategy can be seen in Activity 17, Materials Sort.

Sentence cards

This approach combines elements of matching and sequencing. It is a more structured form of the concept sentences strategy. Simple sentences are cut into 2 or more parts, and muddled up. The children are asked to re-form the broken sentences into more sensible statements. As they discuss the possibilities, they need to explain their thinking and may change their ideas. Mismatches can sometimes cause great hilarity. Any lack of agreement may lead to further research.

When they are familiar with the strategy, children can create sentence cards for others to use. The sentences below are one example of a set created by a group of 6 and 7 year-old children for their classmates to use. A Sentence Cards example can be seen in Activity 4, Blindfold Challenge.

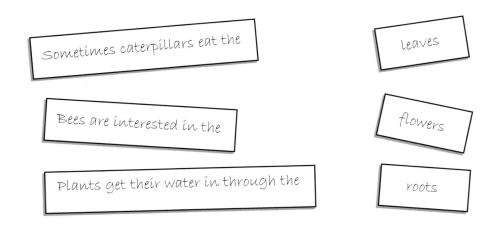

Sequencing

Sequencing is frequently used with young learners. It involves putting a set of photographs, drawings or sentences in a logical order. Having a tangible resource to move around is helpful. Justifying their reasons for a particular sequence helps children to develop their skills of explanation. Being uncertain about a sequence may encourage children to do more finding out and develop their ideas further.

For example, they could sequence the stages of an ice cube melting or a cake being made. They could use the same strategy to plot an interesting route around a habitat, using drawings or photographs of a known area. An example of Sequencing can be seen in Activity 22, Where is Benny?

SPLAT!

This thinking skills version of Bingo! for teams can be organised in a number of ways. You start by organising a 'wall' made up of a variety of words or pictures. This wall can be on a blackboard, a whiteboard, printed onto paper, or even small card grids shared between children on each table.

Each team selects a 'splatter'. You read out a description or definition. Whoever 'splats' their hand over the correct word or picture on the grid wins a point for their team. Children can be encouraged to explain their choice to the rest of the class. Any word that all the children are unsure about can be left to one side for further exploration after the game. An example of Splat! can be seen in Activity 12, Make Me a Duck.

Taboo

This card game causes lots of giggles and has a tendency to be noisy, but is very good for promoting creative thinking. A card is given to one child in each group. This card contains one word in large bold letters at the top. This is the word that is to be guessed. Underneath this word are 3 or 4 more words and these cannot be spoken either. The person with the card can say anything they want, except the words on the card. For example:

potato
mash   chips   spuds

In this example, none of the words that are written on the card can be spoken but a child can say, "It's a vegetable, it grows under the ground", and so on. It's a good idea for you to demonstrate how it is played once or twice, before handing it over to the children. Very young children may not have the self-control to play the game without an adult as guide. An example of Taboo can be seen in Activity 10, Fruit and Veg.

Thinking mat

A thinking mat is a good way to encourage children to talk together, listen to each other's ideas and reach agreement. For example, you might ask the class, "What would a pet need to be healthy and happy?"

- Children write or draw their ideas on their own sheet of paper, without discussion.
- After a few minutes, small groups join together and are given a sheet of coloured paper as their thinking mat.
- In turn, children describe their ideas to the others.
- A scribe in the group (possibly an adult) jots down on the thinking mat the points where they agree.
- If the group can't agree on any particular point, it isn't added to their thinking mat. These can be noted for further exploration and discussion later.
- The different thinking mats can be collected and compared.

Areas of disagreement can create a series of questions to be explored to support further learning. An example of a Thinking Mat can be seen in Activity 9, Ice Blocks.

Yes/no/maybe so

Yes/no/maybe so is a child-friendly version of true/false statements. Children are asked to discuss a statement, or question, and decide if it is true or false or if the answer is yes, no or maybe so. For example, 'All dogs have 3 legs'. They can use a variety of ways to show their decision, such as Talking thumbs (thumbs up, down, or sideways if they're not sure).

When used at the beginning of a topic, the strategy reveals a lot about their understanding, gets them thinking about the statements and begins the learning process. It can also be a valuable summative assessment tool. An example of Yes/No/Maybe so can be seen in Activity 10, Fruit and Veg.

Whole-parts graphic organiser

Graphic organisers can help to guide children's thinking by providing a visual structure to organise their thoughts. In a whole-parts graphic organiser, the children need to think of the different parts of something and discuss what would happen if a single part were removed or missing. The whole thing, the parts that make it up, and what would happen if a part is missing, form a visual structure, a bit like the roots of a tree.

For example, they might think about the individual parts of a person, and then think about the consequences of the person having no eyes/legs/and so on. They might think about the parts of a house, and then decide what would happen if there was no door/electric plugs/and so on. An example of a Whole-Parts Graphic Organiser can be seen in Activity 19, Quickdraw.

Creating a supportive atmosphere that encourages children's talk

To maximise the benefits provided by science experiences, it is important to create a climate where all children feel comfortable and confident to share their ideas.

Once children understand that you value their attempts at describing and explaining, they are more likely to talk freely. If they can chat with a classmate first or make a group decision, they are less likely to feel 'responsible' and insecure about their remarks.

Here are some ways that I find help to create a supportive climate.

Asking questions

The way questions are asked makes a great difference to how confident children feel. They may feel that the teacher knows already. So, rather than reveal what they really think, they try to produce the words they feel their teacher needs. Many questions that teachers ask are about recalling facts, instead of offering opportunities for children to share and recognise the diversity of their ideas.

It is helpful to model looking for answers to questions, whether or not you know the answer. Why not ask "How many questions can we think of? Let's see how many we can answer together now, and which we will need to find out more about later."

Don't worry if you can't answer all of the children's questions. Where possible let children try to research answers. If there are questions that can't be answered then pop these onto a question board to research later. Don't pretend you know an answer if you don't! Activity 3, Spider includes the use of this strategy.

Talk partners

This is a lovely way to get children talking to each other, in a secure, supported atmosphere. It allows them some thinking time, so they can gather their thoughts about the activity.

At any point in an activity, the children are asked to pair up and talk to their partner for a few minutes. You might say things like:

- "With your talk partner, find 3 things that you liked about this activity", or
- "What do you and your talk partner think is going to happen?"

I sometimes ask them to choose a Whisper Partner rather than a talk partner, if I want to keep the noise down!

After the discussion, children can feed back to the whole class what they decided in their pair. In this way they don't have that awful feeling of being put on the spot, and will be more inclined to speak. Talk Partners is used in Activity 11, Up and Down.

Pair, share, square

This is a natural follow on from Talk partners.

- Two children speak together about a given topic.
- This pair then joins a second pair.
- They all share their ideas about the topic.

If you have asked each pair to come up with two points, you might ask the group to find three ideas to feed back to the rest of the class. The children are likely to feel safer in a small group, they can listen to other ideas, and discuss the range of ideas before deciding on their answer. Pair, Share, Square is outlined in Activity 11, Up and Down.

Peer assessment

Whenever children share their ideas with each other, there will be some self and peer assessment going on. I find that it is valuable to give the children time to reflect on each other's work. You can do this by:

- Starting the process for the children. "I thought it was really helpful when Brian and Jaz told us about how they measured how far the cars rolled. What did you think was helpful? Think about it in your own head for one minute first."
- Saving samples of draft work from children elsewhere, so that they can get used to commenting on what their peers are doing.
- Asking children to give a star and a wish – something that is good and something to develop. "I like the way you've drawn the spider really big so I can see the parts clearly. Can you do the same with the worm too?"

You need to handle this sensitively, to help every child to feel comfortable with the outcome. By getting children to make a comment about someone else's work, you help them to start to reflect on their own work too. An example of Peer Assessment is outlined in Activity 19, Quickdraw.

Talking thumbs

Children are asked to consider a comment or question. They might talk about it with their Talk partner. They show what they think by using their thumbs - yes (thumbs up), no (thumbs down) or maybe (thumbs sideways).

This is similar to the Traffic lights cards:

- "Show me green if you understand."
- "Show me orange if you're not sure."
- "Show me red if you would like me to repeat it or if you need some help."

An example of this activity is outlined in Activity 13, Liquid Layers.

Coming to you soon

Children are given advance notice that they will need to talk. You might say "In two minutes, I'm going to ask you to tell us what you know about how seeds grow. Have a quick chat to get ready to tell us your ideas." This allows children to share ideas and be ready with an answer when asked. An example of this strategy is outlined in Activity 13, Liquid Layers.

No hands up

You can tell the class that you intend to ask them some questions, but you don't want to see any hands up. This might seem counterintuitive. The problem with raising hands is that some children tend to dominate, while others can remain disengaged. By using no hands up, all the children are expected to be involved in thinking or talking because any of them can be asked for their answer. In this way, the children who don't normally offer answers are more likely to pay attention and be included in the discussion. An example of this strategy is outlined in Activity 13, Liquid Layers.

Phone a friend

Don't take this literally! Phone a friend has entered our vocabulary, and most children have an idea of what it means. When they are not certain about their own answer, encourage them to ask someone else for help. They soon get used to the idea that getting help is co-operation, not cheating. An example of Phone a Friend is outlined in Activity 7, Flitter Jars.

Pass the parcel

In this approach, the children not the teacher select who will reply.

• Ask a question to the class or hand out an object to describe.
• Choose one child to respond, but don't react to their answer.
• Ask that child to choose someone else to answer the same question, offer a description or possibly answer a new question.
• Repeat with the second child.
• Gather ideas on a whiteboard, flipchart or floor book as they talk.

An example of Pass the Parcel can be seen in Activity 4, Blindfold Challenge.

FEELY WALLS

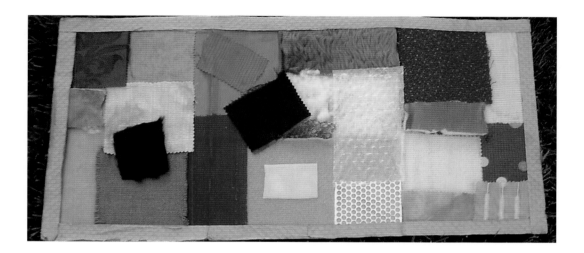

What it is

This activity encourages children to use their sense of touch as they try to identify fabrics hidden inside a Feely Box. The same fabrics are displayed on a 'Feely Wall', and these are used as a comparison when the children are deciding what they can feel inside the box.

Getting started

- ☐ Collect a selection of fabrics of varying texture and thickness. Four or five large pieces for younger children, more for older or higher achieving children.
- ☐ From each sample cut 2 squares of the same size to make 2 identical sets of fabric.
- ☐ Keep one set for the Feely Box and glue the second set to a piece of rigid cardboard or hardboard to make a 'Feely Wall'.

 As well as getting as wide a range of textures as possible, it also helps to choose some fabrics that feel similar to create a greater degree of challenge.

How to use it

Let children touch and talk about the Feely Wall in pairs. Then, taking turns, the children can explore and discuss the fabric in the Feely Box.

After a few minutes, ask if they can match the sample of fabric in the box with one on the Feely Wall, without taking it out of the box.

Allow the children to withdraw the piece of fabric to check it against the fabrics on the Wall.

Start with one sample, or a very small selection of fabrics, in the Feely Box. If you wish to increase the level of demand, put all the samples into the Feely Box or add samples that don't appear on the wall.

Key questions

What does it feel like?

Are there any that feel the same?

Why do you think it is that one?

Can you make up some words to describe it?

Does your partner think it's the same fabric?

Is there one that feels like this?

Looking for evidence of thinking and learning

In this activity children will have the opportunity to:

- ✓ learn about the nature of materials
- ✓ use and explore the meaning of key vocabulary – feel, touch, texture, senses, material, fabric, similar, different
- ✓ describe simple features of materials
- ✓ use simple criteria to sort materials
- ✓ use their sense of touch to describe similarities and differences
- ✓ use language to describe and talk about their experiences.

They can do this by:

- ✓ using their sense of touch to explore, compare and match hidden fabrics with fabrics on the Feely Wall
- ✓ discussing their ideas with each other and their teacher
- ✓ comparing and contrasting and/or grouping materials.

You should see evidence of their thinking and learning in:

- ✓ the way that they respond to questions
- ✓ the way that they talk about the materials
- ✓ how they compare and contrast materials
- ✓ how they classify and group fabrics
- ✓ how they engage in the activity
- ✓ how much they can do without help.

Do not assume that children have an underdeveloped ability to make observations using their senses, simply because they do not match every fabric. If you have chosen a challenging range of fabrics, then they are likely to get some of the matches wrong.

I think it's this furry one 'cos it feels like my cat.

I think it's this flowery one 'cos it's soft and thin.

Extending the activity

Children will learn to think more carefully about criteria, and the relationship between the fabrics, by working in pairs to group the fabrics. "Why have you put those fabrics together?" Ask them to try to give reasons for their choices. Alternatively, you could set criteria and ask the children to "Find me all the furry fabrics … all the shiny fabrics …all the stretchy fabrics." Are all the children able to group the fabrics? Do some children need to see you modelling the process of classifying, to help them to progress?

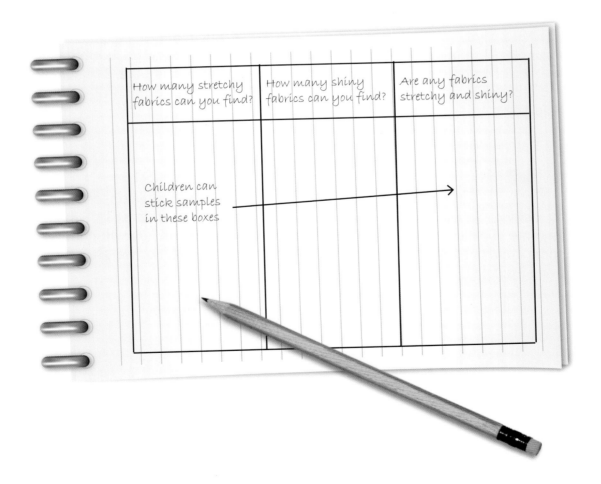

Compare and contrast

Encourage children to make more detailed comparisons between fabrics by talking together about a compare and contrast graphic organiser. Remind them to think about what's the same and what's different. For example, they could make comparisons between a thick woollen fabric and a thin plasticised fabric in terms of absorbency, transparency, strength, texture, etc. Do some children offer very limited comparisons? Which key vocabulary could you use to help them?

Observe, predict, observe, explain

This strategy will help them to think more systematically and justify their choices. "Feel the fabric in the box. Can you find one like it on the Feely Wall? Look at the fabric and see if you are right. Can you tell me how you decided?" A child might respond, for example, "I think it's this pink one 'cos it feels soft and a bit bobbly like the towel to dry my hands. Oh! I was wrong. This one is blue. It's lumpy and a bit rougher." Do some children find this process difficult? Does it help them to see you model this process?

Moving from describing to explaining

Encourage children to move beyond using simple descriptions by asking "Why do you think that?" For example, "It's soft." might become "I think it's this furry one. It feels like my cat." Do all children seem comfortable justifying their ideas? Does modelling the use of the word 'because' help them?

BUBBLE
BUBBLE

What it is

This activity engages both children and adults! It allows children to observe an air bubble travelling through different liquids. They see how this varies, depending on how thick (viscous) the liquid is. They are encouraged to try to explain their observations.

Getting started

- Collect a set of liquids to compare, such as water, golden syrup, washing-up liquid, bubble bath and olive oil. Think about colour, transparency and runniness (viscosity).
- Half fill a set of small bowls with each of the liquids.
- Collect a set of plastic tubes/screw top jars. Long thin ones are the best. Disposable bottles of shampoo etc (from places such as hotels) work really well.
- Put one liquid into each individual tube or jar, leaving a small air gap at the top that will create a bubble when the tube or jar is inverted. You may want to glue the lids on!

Be aware that glass jars present a hazard if breakages occur. Remind children that some liquids are very dangerous.

How to use it

Give the children a chance to explore the liquids by stirring them in the bowls. They can feel how the liquids are different and get an idea of the force needed to stir the liquid in each bowl. Good observation is encouraged from the beginning. It is at this stage that children are 'learning through their fingers.' Encourage lots of talk.

Let each group explore one or two tubes at a time, tilting the tubes up and down, to observe the bubble travelling through the liquid. Respond positively when they first notice the bubble to enhance the feeling of excitement – "Wow! Look at that! Where did that come from?" You can ask the children to race the bubbles and put them into rank order or simply put them into fast and slow groups.

A Reception class was asked the question "Why do you think the bubble goes faster in the water than in the golden syrup?" A child replied, "When I stirred the water it was easy. When I stirred the syrup, I had to push really hard, so I think the bubble has to push hard too." - an excellent response. Could she have explained it so well if she had only had the experience of looking at the tubes?

Key questions

What's happening in that tube when you tip it up?

Is it the same in the other tube?

Which bubbles go quickly / slowly fastest / slowest?

Why do you think the bubble goes faster in the water than in the golden syrup?

Looking for evidence of thinking and learning

In this activity children will have the opportunity to:

✓ learn that liquids are different and behave in different ways

✓ use and explore the meaning of key vocabulary – liquid, transparent, thickness, runniness, bubbles, slower, quicker

✓ describe similarities and differences

✓ think about what might happen before they try something out

✓ understand how science relates to their everyday lives

✓ group and order things using simple, observable features and properties.

They can do this by:

✓ exploring the thickness of each liquid and how hard it is to stir it

✓ trying to predict how different liquids will behave

✓ watching air bubbles move through the liquids

✓ racing the bubbles and sequencing the liquids

✓ making lists, annotating drawings and comparing and contrasting.

You should see evidence of their thinking and learning in:

✓ the way that they respond to questions

✓ how confidently they describe, classify and sequence various liquids

✓ the lists that they make of the liquids that they know

✓ how they explain their predictions and think about what happened

✓ what they put in their annotated drawings and their compare and contrast graphic organisers

✓ how they engage in the activity

✓ how much they can do without help.

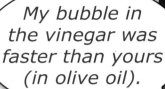

> My bubble in the vinegar was faster than yours (in olive oil).

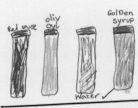

> I can make the bubble stop in the middle.

> This washing up liquid feels like the bubble bath did.

Extending the activity

How many liquids do you know?
How runny are they?

very runny

thick

Total =

STRATEGY:

making a list

Ask the children to think of all the liquids that they know. Encourage them to think about those they have seen outside school as well as in school. They can draw or write these down independently. Alternatively, you can work with groups, or the whole class, to produce a shared class list. Are they able to think of many liquids? Does going on a liquid hunt in magazines and elsewhere help to extend their range of ideas?

Extending the activity cont.

Compare and contrast

Using a compare and contrast graphic organiser encourages children to observe the liquids more carefully. "Can you think what is similar and different about these two liquids? What about the colour, smell, runniness, how quickly the bubble moves?" (See also racing liquids.) What vocabulary do the children use? Does using some key words, real and imaginary, help children to take their ideas forward?

Classifying and grouping / Sequencing

A focus on the speed of movement of the bubble in the tubes helps children to develop their ability to group, classify and sequence. "Which of these liquids are similar? Can you put them in order from the fastest to the slowest?" Are some children uncertain about how to group or make a sequence? Does spending more time exploring some liquids, and modelling creating sequences with them, help?

Observe, predict, observe, explain

Can children build on what they've learned? Try giving the children two new liquids to stir and ask them to predict which bubble will travel faster. "Now watch what happens. Is that what you thought would happen? Why do you think it was different from what you said?" Does exploring the liquids some more help to improve the reliability of their predictions?

Annotated drawing

Asking pupils to annotate their drawings often reveals even more about their understanding. "Those are wonderful drawings of the liquids, let's see if we can add some words." They might name the liquids and add describing words such as thick, thin, slimy, slippery, heavy etc. Are there words that some children are unsure about? Do they use vocabulary creatively? Does making up describing words for one of the liquids help?

SPIDER

What it is

Digital microscopes are commonly available in primary schools. They often hide in cupboards or are used mainly with older children. Their potential for improving observational skills is enormous, as the case study on the following page shows.

Getting started

- ☐ Install the microscope software on your computer. The microscope should then respond as soon as you switch it on.
- ☐ Explore all the features of the microscope such as magnification, taking photos or videos, morphing images, etc.
- ☐ Identify some minibeasts, or small objects, to look at.
- ☐ Ensure that children realise that minibeasts are small animals (invertebrates).

If you use minibeasts please treat them with respect and return them safely to their habitat. Do not leave them under the microscope light for more than a few minutes.

How to use it

A case study:
A reception class was about to embark on the topic of 'Minibeasts'. Their teacher was keen to improve their observational skills in science. The children collected some small creatures from their school grounds and made observational drawings. They were not helped to make these records.

Three weeks later the digital microscope was used to project magnified images of living creatures onto a whiteboard.

The children watched a greatly magnified spider moving around the screen and talked about questions raised by the teacher and other children. In this case, the spider was clearly displaying an egg sac. The class was encouraged to look very carefully at all aspects of the enlarged image of the spider.

The children then made further drawings of their minibeasts and compared their own 'before' and 'after' attempts. There was a marked difference from their earlier attempts. The children could also see the improvement in their drawings.

Key questions

What do you see when we magnify the spider?

What can you tell me about the spider's legs?

What can you tell me about its body?

What else can you see? What questions do you have about it?

Looking for evidence of thinking and learning

In this activity children will have the opportunity to:

✓ learn about minibeasts and identify features of living things

✓ use and explore the meaning of key vocabulary – **minibeast, animals, spiders, insects, living things, body parts** e.g. **antennae, head,** etc

✓ learn the importance of treating living things with care

✓ look closely at similarities and differences

✓ raise questions

✓ learn how to find information

✓ reflect on their work and think about ways that it can be improved.

They can do this by:

✓ collecting and observing small creatures from their local environment

✓ observing the magnified image of a minibeast

✓ using a range of resources to research a variety of minibeasts

✓ comparing **drawings** of the minibeasts and **annotating** them

✓ completing the **KWHL grid**, with help if they need it

✓ discussing **yes/no/maybe** so statements.

You should see evidence of their thinking and learning in:

✓ the way that they respond to questions

✓ the difference between what they draw at the beginning and later

✓ the way that they **annotate** or talk about their **drawings**

✓ the ideas that they want to put on the **KWHL grid**

✓ how they respond to the **yes/no/maybe** so statements

✓ how they engage in the activities

✓ what they can do without help.

Sara's initial drawings of a spider and a worm.

This spider seems to owe more to the Little Miss Muffet nursery rhyme pictures than to what was seen in reality.

The worm is sausage-like but it does have its segments noted along its length.

Three weeks later, Sara draws a spider and a worm again.

This spider has 2 parts to its body, 8 legs and claspers, 'feelers', 8 eyes and an egg sac.

The drawing of the worm shows improvement too. An attempt is made to record the saddle and stiff hairs or setae along the body.

It appears also that Sara has attempted to show how the worm's body becomes quite thin in places as it moves itself along.

Extending the activity

A KWHL grid can be created by you and completed by individuals and groups as they move through the topic. This can be used to encourage children to raise their own questions. In the case study above, children asked questions that they wanted answering about spiders, and the teacher showed them how to find out using a big book format and a computer. Are some children uncertain about creating questions and finding out ideas? Do question starters such as "I wonder where...?", "What would happen if ...?" help them?

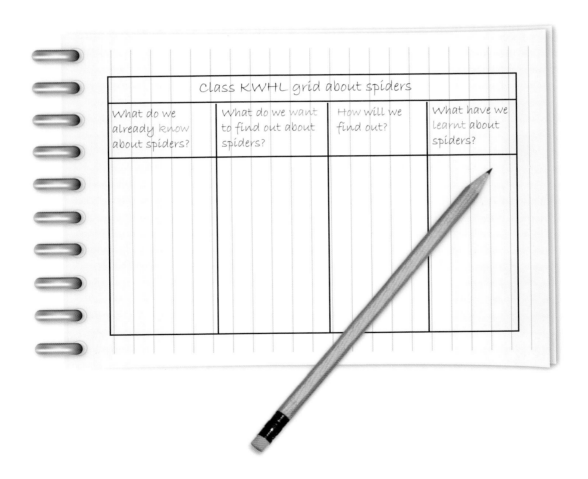

Extending the activity cont.

Annotated drawing

Children can make great strides in their recorded observations if they are encouraged to write ideas alongside their drawings. In some cases you might need to do this for them following discussion. Here, the children could describe parts of the spider's body in great detail. Lewis said, "Miss, the spider's got hairy legs like me!" Are there things that they are not sure about? Does taking another look help them?

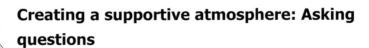

Yes/no/maybe so

Use yes/no/maybe so statements in paired discussion at the start so that you, and the children, will find out what they know about spiders. Do it at the end and you have a quick assessment activity. For example, "All spiders have 6 legs." "Spiders don't have hair." "Spider legs are straight." Are there statements that surprised them? Does looking in books or on the computer help them to find out more?

Splat!

Here, one child from each group has to guess which animal – from a list on the board - is being described by the teacher. When they think they know, they run to the word and 'splat' their hand over it. They then have to explain why they have chosen this animal. Do they need more information to work it out?

Creating a supportive atmosphere: Asking questions

This is an ideal activity to help children to support each other in developing their questioning skills. You can say "Talk to your buddy about what you see. How many questions can we think of? Let's see how many we can answer together now, and which we will need to find out more about later." Don't worry if you cannot answer all of the children's questions. Where possible, let children try to research answers. If there are questions that can't be answered then pop these on a question board to research later. Don't pretend you know an answer if you don't!

BLINDFOLD CHALLENGE

4

What it is

A simple activity that provokes lots of thinking, talking and giggles. It also encourages children to use senses, other than sight, for their observations. This activity will raise children's awareness of how we use and depend on all of our senses. Both the volunteer and the audience become intrigued by how quickly it is possible to identify an object when it is not visible.

One child is blindfolded and has to guess what is put into their open hands, without any hints from other children.

Getting started

☑ Collect examples of interesting objects to try, such as:

   A soft teddy bear   A bar of soap   A slipper
   A box of pencils   A stiff hair brush
   A tube of Smarties with the ends sealed

☑ Find some blindfolds - scarves or soft cloths are fine. Make sure that they are clean.

 Some children are afraid of blindfolds. You need to decide how to deal with this in advance. Allowing them to watch other children first can be helpful.

How to use it

In a small group ask one child to volunteer to be blindfolded. A woolly scarf is usually suitable. The volunteer sits with hands held out awaiting a surprise object. The audience needs to resist giving clues to the volunteer.

The child feels the object for a few moments before deciding what it might be. The child is encouraged to use the sense of smell, in addition to touch, to help to decide. Before they say what they think it is, encourage them to say how it feels, sounds and smells.

Children often deduce the object as soon as they have it in their hands. This astounds their classmates and leads to lively debate about peeping and cheating. The usefulness of the other senses becomes obvious too. A tube of Smarties is usually identified by touch, but children also say they recognise the sound, when they shake the tube.

More mature children can play this game in pairs or small groups, then share ideas with the class about which things were hard to identify and which were easy, and why. NB The game can also be played in reverse with children describing an object to a blindfolded classmate.

Key questions

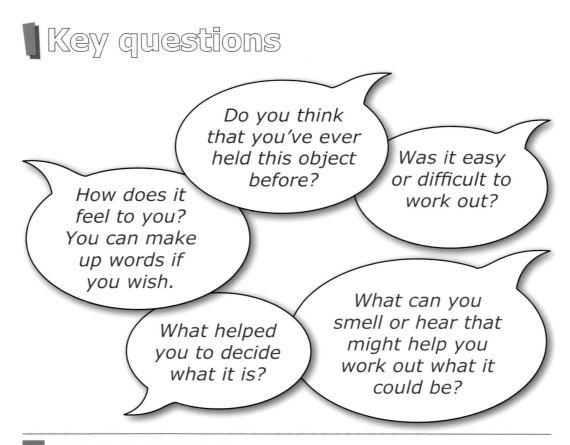

Do you think that you've ever held this object before?

Was it easy or difficult to work out?

How does it feel to you? You can make up words if you wish.

What helped you to decide what it is?

What can you smell or hear that might help you work out what it could be?

Looking for evidence of thinking and learning

In this activity children will have the opportunity to:

- ✓ learn about the importance of their senses and how to make effective use of them
- ✓ use and explore the meaning of key vocabulary – senses, touch, feel, sight, see, smell, sound, hear, similar, different, texture
- ✓ explore and identify objects by touch, smell and hearing
- ✓ apply everyday experience to new situations
- ✓ identify similarities and differences
- ✓ listen to, and value, each other's ideas.

They can do this by:

- ✓ watching each other trying to identify objects without seeing them
- ✓ trying to identify the objects themselves
- ✓ playing the sentence card game
- ✓ using the whole-parts relationship graphic organiser to think about the importance of their senses.

You should see evidence of their thinking and learning in:

- ✓ the way that they respond to questions
- ✓ the words that they use to describe the objects
- ✓ their ability to match the sentence cards with or without help
- ✓ what they put in the graphic organiser about senses
- ✓ how they engage in the activities
- ✓ what they can do without help.

> I think it is a teddy because I can feel its arms and legs and it is squishy.

> It feels smooth...and it smells ....It's soap!

> Oooh! This feels hard and prickly ... like a hedgehog.

Extending the activity

Create sentences and then cut up the beginnings and endings. Children are challenged to work out which bits go together. They can have fun mixing them up and talking about what the problems would be if, for example, a teddy was heavy, hard, stiff and prickly. More confident learners can start with beginnings of sentences and think of ways of finishing them with, or without, some key words on cards. Are all children confident about their ideas? Does it help to explore the objects some more?

STRATEGY:
Sentence cards

? ! ? IS...   HEAVY

HARD   SQUISHY

SOFT

The soap is

The teddy bear is

The hairbrush is

The ruler is

The rubber band is

soft, furry and squashable.

light, stretchy and smooth.

heavy, hard, stiff and prickly.

smooth, scented and can be scratched.

light, bendy, smooth and plastic.

Whole-parts graphic organiser

Help the children to understand more about their senses by using a simple graphic organiser to collect their ideas. "What are our senses? How does each one help us? What would it be like if one sense was taken away?" Use the discussion to think about how blind or deaf people manage to live safely and successfully. Are there more things that they would like to know? Does meeting a visually or hearing impaired person, or looking in books or on the internet, help?

Creating a supportive atmosphere: Thinking time and Peer assessment

This is an ideal activity to illustrate how you can help children to understand the value of giving thinking time and responding positively to their peers' ideas. It is all too easy for them to tell their classmate the answer before the child has had time to think. Whether they are working with or without you, encouraging children to allow time for thinking about the object will help them to value each other's thinking. Giving a positive response to the ideas that are put forward is important in helping all children to feel that their ideas are worthwhile.

Creating a supportive atmosphere: Pass the parcel

This is also an ideal activity to illustrate how pass the parcel can encourage children to share their ideas. When the children have explored a range of everyday objects, remove all the objects. Ask one child to imagine the object, such as a pineapple, and think of words to describe it, using all of the senses.

This child then chooses a classmate and asks if they agree with the chosen adjectives and if they would use any extra words to describe a pineapple. Subsequent children can also be asked to contribute and you can collate all ideas together on a whiteboard, flip chart or floor book.

You could then pass the object round to see how closely their words match the real object. What words would they now like to add?

DRAWING PARTNERS

5

What it is

When asked to draw something, children often draw what they think is there, not what is in front of them. If we can encourage them to really look at what they are observing, their results will be much improved.

In this activity, young children are asked to look closely at, and sketch, a partner's face. Children involved in this activity are astounded by how much better their work is after they have observed carefully. Daniel said, "I didn't know I could draw!"

Getting started

- ☐ Collect some drawing materials.
- ☐ Make, or find, some viewing windows – small rectangular windows that allow the user to focus on what can be seen just through the cut out part.
- ☐ Mirrors could also be useful.

 Take care if using glass mirrors. Plastic ones are available, although they may not give such a high quality image.

How to use it

A case study:
In this class, the children were asked to work in pairs and draw each other - little initial guidance was given.

After 10 minutes, the teacher collected the work in and then called one boy to the front of the class. She asked the class to look very carefully at his features and guided them to focus on eye shape, position of ears, hair texture, etc.

Pairs then did a second drawing of each other. Afterwards they were able to compare the first and second sketch and talk about improvements.

Over the next 10 days, children also used viewing windows, which allowed them to focus on one feature at a time, such as the eye or the mouth. A third and final drawing was made and then the children could review their work overall.

You can encourage children to think by comparing the drawing of themselves and what they see when they look in a mirror.

Key questions

Look at Daniel's eyes. Most of you have drawn a circle for the eyes. Are eyes really round?

Did you put eyebrows and eyelashes in your drawings?

Can you see the shape of Daniel's chin?

Does his hair grow away from his forehead or towards it?

Looking for evidence of thinking and learning

In this activity children will have the opportunity to:

- ✓ learn to recognise and compare similarities and differences between themselves and their classmates
- ✓ use and explore the meaning of key vocabulary – detail, observe, face, nose, eyes, eyebrows, nostrils
- ✓ observe closely and focus on detail
- ✓ communicate their observations through simple drawings
- ✓ reflect on their work and seek to improve it
- ✓ respect each other.

They can do this by:

- ✓ taking time to observe a classmate closely and recording their observations through talking and drawing
- ✓ looking at their own faces, comparing them with the drawings of their faces and talking about how their work and their classmates' work can be improved
- ✓ annotating their drawings
- ✓ responding to yes/no/maybe so statements.

You should see evidence of their thinking and learning in:

- ✓ the way that they respond to questions
- ✓ how they talk about their drawings and those of their classmates
- ✓ the improvement in their drawings during the activity
- ✓ how they annotate their drawings of faces
- ✓ their answers in the yes/no/maybe so game
- ✓ how they engage in the activities
- ✓ what they can do without help.

What children do and say

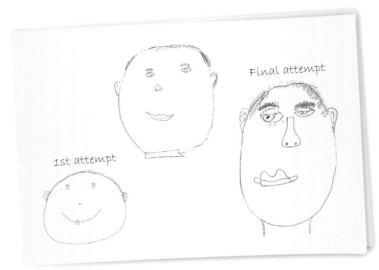

"Carly's hair is very curly ... not like mine."

"Eyebrows are made of little hairs!"

"The tops of my ears are as high as my eyebrows!"

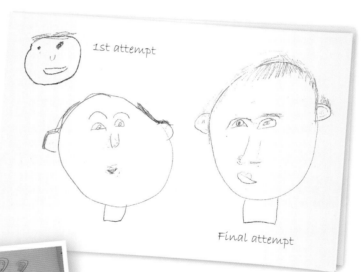

The viewing window has been used here to encourage the child to focus on her partner's eyes, lips, nose and ears.

Following this, the child made the final sketch.

Extending the activity

Children will make great strides in their recorded observations if they are encouraged to write extra information alongside their drawings. In some cases you can do this for them following discussion. In the example, the children described how their work improved, once they had taken time to make good observations of their partner.

STRATEGY:
Annotated drawing

Teacher: "Look carefully at your drawing. Choose a few things in the drawing that are important and tell me (or your classmate) about them. I have started some sentences to help you."

Yes/no/maybe so

Do this quickly at the end of the session to help children to think of similarities and differences and to see how well they can spot them. They can respond by holding up cards saying yes/no/maybe so or true/false/it depends. Alternatively, simply putting their thumb up, down or sideways is a quick check of understanding.

> Everyone in our class has blonde hair.
> All faces have ... 2 eyes / 2 ears / 1 pair of eyelashes...
> Most people in our class have brown hair.

I find that most children handle this very confidently. Are there any who find this difficult? Does spending more time looking at, and talking about, faces help them?

Hot seating

Ask a child to volunteer to sit in the hot seat. The volunteer selects a face from a series of coloured photos, or paintings, of famous faces which you have collected and put on display. Alternatively, ask them to think of a member of the class. Other children have to guess which person they are thinking of, as quickly as possible. Individuals can ask a question but the volunteer can only respond with "yes" or "no". Classmates might ask," Are you thinking of a girl?" "Does she have black hair?" "Are her eyes blue?" "Does she have freckles?" Care needs to be taken, if using class members, to guide the activity to ensure that questions raised do not upset the person in question.

Creating a supportive atmosphere: Peer assessment

This activity provides an ideal opportunity to encourage children to think about and value each other's ideas.

Create a photo gallery of before and after pictures. Children look at each other's drawings and talk about the improvements that they can see in their classmates' work. They, or you, write these on post-it notes and stick them near the pictures to celebrate each other's achievements. Are all children able to contribute? Does a sentence bank help them?

LET ME OUT!

6

What it is

In this exciting activity children handle a foil-wrapped object. They are encouraged to think about what might be inside. They discuss the possibilities with each other and their teacher. When it's opened up, they find a small figure, such as a Lego® person, trapped inside a block of ice! How can they get him out of his icy prison?

You could even turn this into a news report and weather forecast with spacemen arriving on Earth in giant hailstones!

Getting started

- ☑ Put a small amount of water in a yoghurt pot or similar and add a plastic figure. Put this in the freezer. Try little Santa figures at Christmas time!
- ☑ When it is frozen, top up the water and freeze again so that the figure will be inside the ice, not floating on top.
- ☑ Wrap the ice in foil.
- ☑ Collect some bowls and any other resources that they may request to release the figure, such as little hammers.

 Take care if children do try to hammer the person out. Ice and hammers can both be very mobile!

How to use it

Allow children to handle their own foil parcel; sharing can lead to tears! Scientific vocabulary can be introduced quite naturally into the discussion. They soon notice that the object is cold and their hands start to become wet. Do they know why? Is this a clue to what's inside?

You can ask them to bang the foil parcel on the table, so they find out that it is also hard - you can ask them if it will bend or stretch. I have great fun by lifting an ice parcel to my ear, shushing the children and pretending that I can hear a voice inside calling, 'Let me out!'

Once they have unwrapped the ice, and the noise has subsided, you can start some problem solving. How can they get the little person out of the ice block? They'll probably suggest teeth or hammers at first! Let the children safely explore as many of their own ideas as possible before you add any ideas.

NB Providing bowls of tepid water or holding the block under a running tap melts the ice very quickly.

Key questions

Where do you think this water is coming from?

Why are your hands cold and wet?

What will make the ice melt?

How can we get the person out of the ice?

Would anything make the ice melt faster?

Looking for evidence of thinking and learning

In this activity children will have the opportunity to:

- ✓ learn about the properties of water and that it freezes and melts
- ✓ use and explore the meaning of key vocabulary – ice, melt, freeze, thaw, water, liquid, solid
- ✓ use their everyday experience to make predictions
- ✓ solve problems
- ✓ carry out investigations and compare what happened with what they expected to happen
- ✓ communicate their ideas through writing or drama.

They can do this by:

- ✓ playing with the ice parcel and working out what it might be
- ✓ exploring ways of getting the person out of the ice
- ✓ comparing different ways of melting the ice and creating a sequence of drawings of the ice melting and the person escaping
- ✓ creating a story about the people escaping from the ice.

You should see evidence of their thinking and learning in:

- ✓ the way that they respond to questions
- ✓ the language that they use to describe their observations
- ✓ the ideas that they try out and what they say is happening
- ✓ the comparisons that they make between ways of helping the person to escape
- ✓ the sequence of drawings of ice melting
- ✓ what they include in their stories or plays
- ✓ how they engage in the activities
- ✓ what they can do without help.

What children do and say

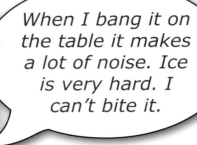

When I bang it on the table it makes a lot of noise. Ice is very hard. I can't bite it.

My hand's getting all wet. My shirt is wet. It's coming out of the ice.

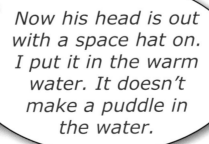

Now his head is out with a space hat on. I put it in the warm water. It doesn't make a puddle in the water.

Extending the activity

At the start	After . . . .

After	At the end

STRATEGY:

Sequencing

Once the children have explored lots of ideas for helping the little person to escape, you can give them another one to observe more carefully. They can choose which they think will be the fastest way out, e.g. in a bowl of warm water or placed on the window sill. They record what happens through a series of drawings or photographs, showing how much ice has melted after 5 minutes, 15 minutes, and so on. It may take some time depending on where it is. Were there some things that happened that surprised them? Are there new questions to be answered?

Compare and contrast

It is enjoyable and challenging for children to compare and contrast different possibilities for melting the ice, such as putting it in cold water or warm water, on a radiator or in a dark cold place, in a fridge or leaving it in the room, etc. They could draw pictures to show the differences. Are there new questions to be answered?

Create a story

Let Me Out! lends itself to a variety of storylines. Perhaps the little people have travelled to Earth through space in their ice rockets? Maybe they were caught in a storm and fell to the ground in giant hailstones?

Encourage the children to act out the journey to Earth with appropriate sounds and movements. They could also consider that, once out of their ice rockets, it might be that the spacemen don't eat the same food as humans. What on Earth could they eat? Give children an opportunity to create story lines by drawing or writing.

Are you able to record and watch the plays? Do they give the children new ideas to add to their stories?

Creating a supportive atmosphere: Pair, share, square

This is an ideal opportunity to help the children to learn how to share ideas. When they have finished exploring ways of helping their own person to escape, encourage them to work with a partner to share what happened. Which ways helped and which didn't work so well and why? Then get that pair to join up with another pair. Can they create a list of all the ways that helped the person to escape? You can then gather these together and use this as a lead into investigating some things more carefully.

FLITTER JARS

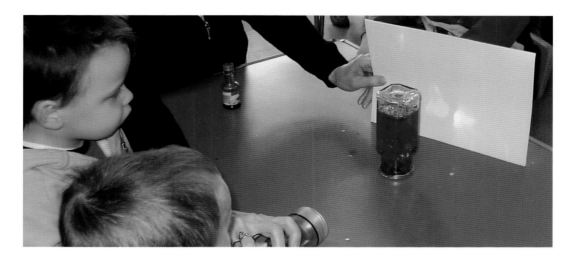

7

What it is

This activity mimics the Snow or Flitter Domes, popular since Victorian times, which contain objects in a swirling snowstorm. This highly engaging activity encourages children to talk about light, shadows and materials. It can lead naturally into children spinning and twirling about in P.E. like the pieces of flitter in the jars.

Getting started

- ☑ Gather a selection of transparent containers with lids.
- ☑ Collect tiny pieces of foil, coloured glitter, table confetti, etc (the flitter).
- ☑ Choose some food colourings.
- ☑ Find torches and check that the lights are bright.
- ☑ Collect white paper to act as mini screens.

 Smooth-sided glass jars produce better shadows in this activity but they present a hazard if breakages occur.

How to use it

Let children choose a jar from the ones provided and fill it with water. You might want to get them to pop the lid on until they have decided what to add.

Give children time to explore the shiny glittery bits to decide which they would like to add to the jar. Encourage them to observe closely as the glitter is added. Less is more in this activity - small amounts of foil and glitter produce much clearer results than shovelfuls of shine!

Let them try the jars with clear water first. Finally, a few drops of food colour will enliven the concoction ... and their Flitter Jars are ready to use!

Let children have time to enjoy tipping the jar back and forth repeatedly to watch the movement of the shiny pieces. Compare the movements caused by a big shake, a little shake and just tipping the jar.

Shine a torch through the moving liquid and allow the shadows and colours to fall onto a piece of white paper or screen behind the jar. Compare different jars. This will fascinate your children.

Key questions

What do you see when you add the shiny pieces to the water?

How can you make the pieces move faster?

In what ways can you change the shadows?

What can you see when you shine the light?

Looking for evidence of thinking and learning

In this activity children will have the opportunity to:

- ✓ learn about shadows and how they are formed
- ✓ use and explore the meaning of key vocabulary – liquid, patterns, shadows, light, movement, change
- ✓ make and explore an object and observe it closely
- ✓ explore phenomena and look for patterns and change
- ✓ describe, talk about and record what they observe
- ✓ be aware of cause and effect
- ✓ offer explanations.

They can do this by:

- ✓ selecting the ingredients and making their own Flitter Jar
- ✓ finding ways to change the movement of the flitter in the jars and the shadows
- ✓ shining the light through different Flitter Jars and using the torch to create shadows
- ✓ comparing Flitter Jars and annotating drawings of them
- ✓ generating instructions for how to make a Flitter Jar.

You should see evidence of their thinking and learning in:

- ✓ how they respond to questions
- ✓ what they observe
- ✓ what they do to change the movement of the flitter and the shadows
- ✓ how they annotate or talk about their drawings
- ✓ the ideas that they want to include in the graphic organiser
- ✓ the set of instructions they create and how they talk about them
- ✓ how they engage in the activities
- ✓ how much they can do without help.

Extending the activity

With support, young children can review what they've learned by discussing or creating a set of instructions for making a Flitter Jar. The instructions can be cut into strips. The children can work individually or, preferably, as a small group to sort them into the correct sequence. In this activity there could be more than one appropriate sequence.

STRATEGY:
Set of instructions

This is how to make a Flitter Jar.

Find a clear jar.

Almost fill the jar with water.

Choose some shiny bits.

Put the shiny bits into the jar.

Add 3 drops of food colouring to the water.

Put the lid on the jar and screw it on tightly.

Shake the jar and watch all the shiny bits float around.

Shine a torch into the jar and watch the shadows dance.

 ### Compare and contrast

Encourage children to observe more closely and talk about their ideas by getting pairs of children to compare and contrast their own Flitter Jar with a classmate's. You could use a graphic organiser to help them to look at differences in colour, shape of jar, how the pieces inside move, what sort of shadows are made, and so on. Are there new ideas or explorations to try?

 ### Annotated drawing

Encourage children to observe more closely by getting them to draw what they observed while playing with their Flitter Jars. You can add comments to annotate the drawing for them. Some of the older children might be able to annotate their own drawings to describe what they saw inside the Flitter Jar after it was shaken or when they shone a light on it. How confidently are they able to annotate their drawings? Does exploring the Flitter Jars further help them to develop the language they use?

 ### Creating a supportive atmosphere: Phone a friend

This is an ideal opportunity to see how you can help children to build confidence in answering questions by using Phone a friend. Ask one of the children to recall, in the correct order, all of the steps taken to make their Flitter Jar. Alternatively, ask someone to name ten items that they have in their home that would shine (like the flitter does). Are they getting stuck or running out of ideas? They can get support from a friendly classmate by phoning a friend - in other words, choosing someone else to help them to answer the question.

MAPSTICKS

What it is

Mapsticks is based on the Australian Aboriginal idea of journey sticks. They can be used to support mapwork in geography. In science, a Mapstick encourages observational skills, knowledge of habitats and promotes speaking and listening.

The children use twigs, lolly-sticks or lengths of dowelling to record interesting finds as they search an area for a variety of habitats or to observe plants, creatures or materials of interest.

Getting started

- ☐ Collect some wooden lolly-sticks, dowelling or twigs.
- ☐ Gather some wool or coloured sticky labels to use as markers on the stick.
- ☐ Find an outdoor area where there are plants and animals for children to spot. Many playgrounds are richer environments than you might first think.

 Check the school's outdoor working policy. Encourage no fingers in mouths and ensure hands are washed at the end of the activity. This will teach children good habits for when they play in outdoor environments.

How to use it

The strategy can be used in several ways. Groups of children explore the given area with an adult and note any item of interest by making a record on their Mapstick. Some children may work well in pairs.

Small, coloured stickers or strands of coloured wool are attached to the lolly-stick or twig. Each colour represents an observation of interest to the child. Objects, such as flowers, leaves or small stones can be tied or stuck on to the stick, if appropriate. Let children try to do as much as possible on their own.

Once the Mapstick is complete it can be used as an aide-memoire for the children during a speaking and listening exercise.

A simple route around the school grounds can be displayed on the wall using photos of significant areas. Children can begin and end their exploration at any point.

Key questions

How does the stick help you to remember?

Why did you choose those things?

Where did you go and what did you see?

How many different things have you recorded on your Mapstick?

How is your stick different from your partner's stick?

Would it be different at a different time of year?

Looking for evidence of thinking and learning

In this activity children will have the opportunity to:

✓ find out about features of living things in their local environment

✓ use and explore the meaning of key vocabulary – environment, natural, living, dead, colour, plant, animal, flower, leaf, twig

✓ identify similarities and differences

✓ think about ways of systematically recording their ideas

✓ use language to recreate experiences

✓ think about their own safety.

They can do this by:

✓ exploring a route in their school grounds and recording their observations using a Mapstick

✓ talking about their journey with the aid of the Mapstick

✓ comparing their Mapsticks and making lists of what they've seen

✓ talking about and creating yes/no/maybe so statements.

You should see evidence of their thinking and learning in:

✓ how they respond to questions

✓ how they choose what they put on their Mapsticks

✓ the way that they talk about what they have seen

✓ the contents of the lists that they make

✓ how they compare and contrast, and annotate, Mapsticks

✓ how they respond to, and create, yes/no/maybe so statements

✓ how they engage in the activities

✓ what they can do without help.

"Sarah went to the pond and I went to the infant area."

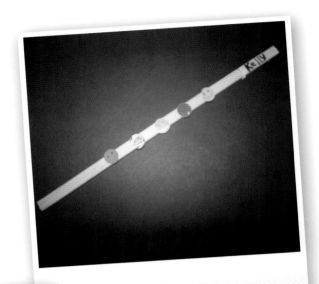

I can remember where I've been and what I've seen when I look at my Mapstick.

"Sarah found a lot more things alive than I did but I did find lots of bright crisp bags."

Extending the activity

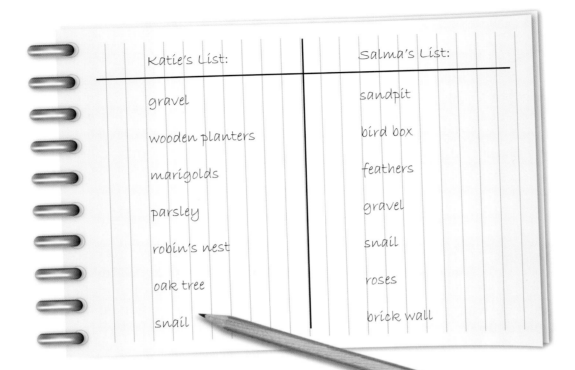

Katie's List:

gravel

wooden planters

marigolds

parsley

robin's nest

oak tree

snail

Salma's List:

sandpit

bird box

feathers

gravel

snail

roses

brick wall

> Can you find some things that both Katie and Salma saw?

> Can you find some things that only Katie saw?

STRATEGY:

Compare and contrast

Using the Talk partners strategy, ask children to compare their list with a classmate. Tell them to note the differences in the plants, animals, materials, etc that they found. Can they find 1 or 2 things that are the same and 1 or 2 that are different in each route? Are they unsure about what they have seen? Does going outside to take another look help?

Making a list

Using the Mapstick as an aide-memoire, children make a list of all the plants, animals or materials that they saw on their particular route. They can use both words and pictures to do this. Encourage them to add details such as what it is (if they know), where it was found or any other details that they can remember. Have they remembered their journey? Does taking another look outside help?

Annotated drawing

Alternatively, the stick can be attached to a piece of card and annotations (words and pictures) added around the stick or information labels can be added to the stick itself. Do they want to take another look outside to remember what things looked like?

Yes/no/maybe so

Using this activity, children can answer true/false questions such as "All the minibeasts were found on leaves." "The best place to find woodlice was on the playground." Are there some statements that surprised them? Does doing some research help them to find out more?

Finally challenge each pair to make up a statement for the rest of the class.

Creating a supportive atmosphere: Pair, share, square

The Yes/no/maybe so strategy provides an ideal opportunity for using the pair, share, square approach to support children in developing their understanding of the environment around them.

ICE BLOCKS

What it is

In my experience, children love handling ice but they rarely have large pieces of it to explore. During this activity, they work with huge ice cubes made in margarine or ice cream tubs.

They discover that even tepid or cold water is able to melt a hole through the ice block in a very short time indeed. This activity could be a good follow-up to Activity 6, Let Me Out!

Getting started

- ☐ Fill large containers with water and put them in the freezer. They may take several days to freeze.
- ☐ Collect some trays or washing up bowls to hold the ice cubes as they melt.
- ☐ Gather some water jugs or watering cans.
- ☐ Have some salt available for those who might want to try it.

 Large blocks of ice are heavy. Ensure that they don't fall onto small toes – perhaps by sitting on the floor to do the activity. Beware - ice straight from the freezer can stick to skin. Do not let children hack at the ice with sharp instruments.

How to use it

Give the children the large pieces of ice and allow plenty of time to experience and explore the ice first. Then you might want to pop the blocks back in the freezer while you are discussing the next stage.

Challenge the children to make a round hole or 'window' in the ice to peep through. You could show them one that you have made and ask them how you did it. You could give them the clue that you used water.

Let children talk to a partner and then discuss their ideas with a bigger group or whole class. Some children may come up with alternatives, such as rubbing the ice or adding salt. It helps to let them explore these ideas too, if it is safe to do so.

Children can work on their own, or with you, and use a plastic jug to pour water onto their ice. They can count the number of jugs used. They could also see if the temperature of the water makes a difference. Encourage them to observe what happens after each jug. The best holes are made if children keep pouring the water on the same point. The children will enjoy exploring this for themselves. A hole appears quite quickly. Children get great enjoyment from peeping at each other through the hole.

Securing their ice windows on a windowsill, particularly on a bright day, provides a very eye-catching resource. Predicting, and then timing, to see how long it takes the block to melt completely, can promote thinking and discussion.

Key questions

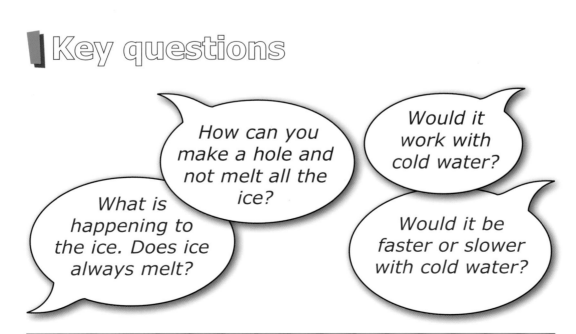

How can you make a hole and not melt all the ice?

Would it work with cold water?

What is happening to the ice. Does ice always melt?

Would it be faster or slower with cold water?

Looking for evidence of thinking and learning

In this activity children will have the opportunity to:

✓ learn about the properties of water and how it changes from solid to liquid

✓ use and explore the meaning of key vocabulary – liquid, water, ice, freeze, melt, hot, cold

✓ begin to offer ideas about how to solve a given problem

✓ test out their ideas

✓ use first hand experience to answer questions

✓ compare what happened with what they expected to happen.

They can do this by:

✓ exploring very large pieces of ice

✓ talking about how to make a hole in the ice and trying out ideas

✓ discussing how different factors affect how ice melts

✓ making predictions about the time needed for ice to melt in different situations

✓ sequencing photos of melting ice or annotating their drawings.

You should see evidence of their thinking and learning in:

✓ the way that they respond to questions

✓ their suggestions of how to make a hole in the ice

✓ how they test their ideas

✓ what they say about the ice melting

✓ how they sequence the photographs or annotate their drawings of melting ice

✓ how they engage in the activity

✓ how much they can do without help.

Don't worry if children do not succeed in making a hole in the ice but have worked very effectively to explore their own ideas. This is still a sign that they are thinking and learning.

"The water's making a hole in my ice block!"

"I can see through the hole and I can see through some bits of the ice too."

Extending the activity

At the beginning, or end, of this activity children could be given a set of photographs, which show a giant ice cube melting. They can discuss the stages and talk about what makes the ice cube melt. Are there any questions that they want to answer now that they have thought about melting ice?

STRATEGY:
Sequencing

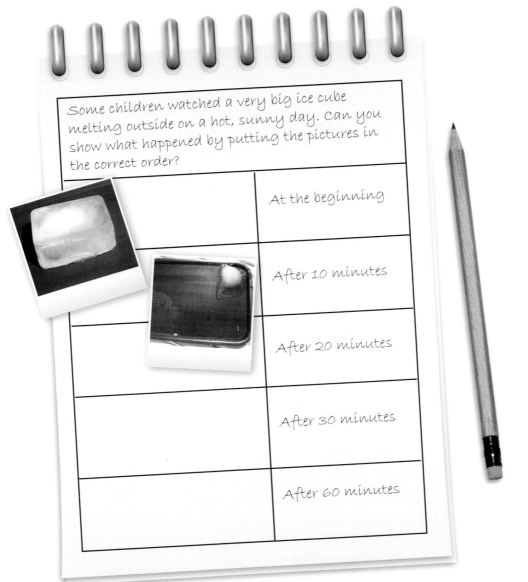

Some children watched a very big ice cube melting outside on a hot, sunny day. Can you show what happened by putting the pictures in the correct order?

	At the beginning
	After 10 minutes
	After 20 minutes
	After 30 minutes
	After 60 minutes

Extending the activity cont.

Annotated drawing

Ask them to draw a series of pictures showing what they think will happen to an ice cube if it's taken out of the freezer and left in a dish for several hours. Encourage them to add comments to their picture on their own, with a partner or with adult help. They can compare this with their observations. Were there some things that surprised them and will they need to explore some more ice to find out answers to their questions?

Thinking mats

Children draw or write what they know about ice on their mat. When they join together in a small group, their ideas can be combined into a simple consensus of what they know between them. Groups can then compare ideas. Are there some things about ice where different children or groups have different ideas? These could be turned into questions to answer. Are there some things that they are not sure about? What would be the best way to find out?

FRUIT AND VEG

10

What it is

Printing with paint and fruit or vegetable pieces is not uncommon in classrooms of young children.

This activity challenges the children to create prints identical to those already created by the teacher. This means that each child has to compare shape, size and colour before they can produce a perfect match. They also will need to look carefully at the structure and what is inside the fruit and vegetables.

Getting started

- ☑ Set up any technique that you normally use for printing.
- ☑ Gather some fruit and vegetables.
- ☑ Make prints of individual fruits and vegetables. If you want to increase the level of demand, cut the fruit and veg in interesting ways, before you make the print.
- ☑ Have suitable knives available to cut the fruit and vegetables.

 Children should not eat any food used for printing or put it in their mouths. Children use knives regularly for cutting food but may need to be supported in cutting hard, raw fruit and vegetables. You need to decide which foods are safe for them to cut alone.

How to use it

Encourage children to look closely at the fruit and vegetables. Can they see any seeds? What is the inside like? Is it juicy, soft or hard? Does cutting it in different ways make a difference to what you see?

Now show the children how to print effectively. For example, you might want them to press fruit or vegetable pieces onto sponges covered in coloured paint before dabbing them onto paper. Allow the children to explore the outcomes of their printing before they go on to the next stage of the activity.

After they have finished exploring, have prints of individual fruits or vegetables prepared on small pieces of paper to give to a child or pair of children. Then ask, "Can you make me one exactly like this one?"

To produce an identical print, children need to consider which fruit or vegetable to select, as well as the paint colour to be used. They need to match shape and size too. They will be able to draw on what they have learnt through their earlier explorations. For example, leeks can be cut crosswise or longitudinally. When cut crosswise, they look very similar to prints from sliced carrots.

Key questions

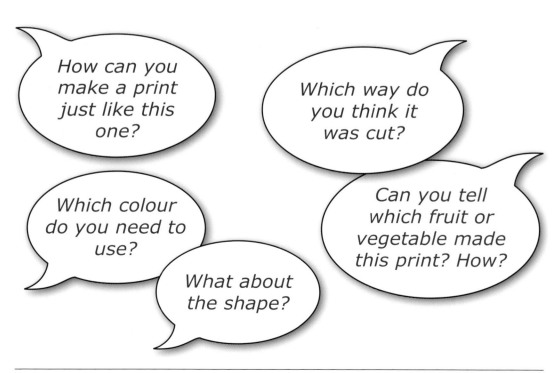

How can you make a print just like this one?

Which way do you think it was cut?

Which colour do you need to use?

What about the shape?

Can you tell which fruit or vegetable made this print? How?

Looking for evidence of thinking and learning

In this activity children will have the opportunity to:

✓ find out about, and identify, some of the features of plants

✓ use and explore the meaning of key vocabulary – **vegetables**, **fruit**, **seeds**, **roots**, **leaves**, **skin**, **peel**, **flesh**, **similar**, **difference**, **pattern**

✓ group things according to observable features

✓ make simple comparisons and identify simple patterns

✓ explore colour, shape and form in two and three dimensions.

They can do this by:

✓ testing printing with different fruits, vegetables and colours

✓ observing the cut surfaces of fruits and vegetables

✓ trying to match their prints to ones made by their teacher

✓ responding to **yes/no/maybe so** statements, creating **lists** of fruit and playing **taboo**

✓ talking about 'The Upside Down Seeds' **Concept Cartoon**.

You should see evidence of their thinking and learning in:

✓ their responses to questions

✓ what they notice and say about fruit and vegetables

✓ the **lists** they make of all the fruits and vegetables that they know

✓ their attempts at replicating the fruit and vegetable prints

✓ the answers that they give in the **yes/no/maybe so** game

✓ the views that they express about the **Concept Cartoon**

✓ how well they engage with the activities

✓ what they can do without help.

"I don't know if this print was made with a plum or a lemon"

"I think it's an apple ...but it's purple!"

"Look! The leek has got lots of little circles inside it!"

Extending the activity

Using a Concept Cartoon, for example 'Upside Down Seeds' from the Science Questions series (Naylor and Naylor, 2000), will encourage children to think about scientific problems, carry out an investigation and find out the answers themselves. Thinking about how plants grow is a natural follow-on to this activity. When they have investigated the problem, are there any more questions to find out about? What might they want to do next?

Extending the activity cont.

Yes/no/maybe so

A very simple version of a True/false game can be played here. For example, "A carrot is blue." "A pineapple is smooth." See the CD for more examples. Teacher: "Thumbs up if what I say is true. Thumbs down if what I say is not true and thumbs sideways if you are not sure." Do all the children agree? Does more finding out help them to make up their minds?

Making a list

Children could use the Pair, share, square approach to begin to make as long a list as possible of all the fruits and vegetables that they know as a stimulus to start the activity. You could link this to the alphabet and look for items that begin with each of the letters of the alphabet. Are they fruit or vegetables? Where do they grow? Do they have seeds? What colour are they? Does doing more finding out help them to build their knowledge?

Classifying and grouping

Give children a small selection of sliced fruit and ask them to think of as many ways as possible to sort them – seeds, colour, texture, shape, etc. Now give them some sliced vegetables and ask them to include those in their groups. Ask them to share the reasons for the groups that they have chosen.

Taboo

One child from each group has a card with the name of a fruit or vegetable at the top. Below this are some words that the child cannot use to describe it. For example, POTATO: chips, mash, spuds. Can the other children guess what it is?

This activity will help them to focus on their knowledge of the actual fruit or vegetable rather than how it is used. How hard is it to talk about the fruit and vegetable without mentioning its use? Are there some that children are not sure about? Does finding out more information help?

UP AND DOWN

11

What it is

Raisins dropped into lemonade will sink and rise continuously until the gas has dispersed from the liquid.

Children love watching this happen. Discussing exactly what they can see can produce a wealth of language and encourage thinking. The focus is on what the children observe, and NOT on scientific explanations involving mass and density.

Getting started

- Buy some cheap bottles of lemonade. Don't use very old lemonade as it might be flat.
- Get some raisins, you might want to find some different kinds to investigate.
- Find some tall, transparent, plastic containers.
- Have some straws or stirrers to hand to help get the gas out of the lemonade.

 If you decide to use glass tumblers, find out about the use of glass in your school. Sweep up any breakages immediately and dispose of carefully to avoid accidents.

How to use it

It is best for the children to work in pairs. Give them a freshly poured tumbler of lemonade. Let the children experience the effect of the gas in the lemonade. If they lean in closely, they will feel the splashes on their faces as the bubbles pop and burst at the surface.

Then drop in 5 or 6 raisins and ask the children to watch carefully and describe what happens. They should see the raisins become covered in gas bubbles and rise to the surface. As the bubbles pop, the raisins drop lower in the liquid. Once they have picked up enough bubbles, they will rise up again. What do they think makes the raisins rise?

Once they have exhausted all of their ideas, ask the children to carefully stir the liquid, until there are no more gas bubbles. Now what's happening? Can anyone explain this?

Most of the raisins will now lie on the bottom of the container, because there are no gas bubbles to carry them to the top. As they have been moving up and down so quickly, some children think that they're alive, even though they saw the raisins at the beginning ... so now that they've stopped moving about, they may think that they're dead!

What constitutes 'being alive' can be discussed quite naturally here.

Key questions

What do the bubbles feel like when they pop on your face?

What can you see in the lemonade?

Why do you think the raisins are going up and down?

What happens if you stir the lemonade?

Looking for evidence of thinking and learning

In this activity children will have the opportunity to:

✓ observe gases in liquids and how gases help things to float

✓ use and explore the meaning of key vocabulary – liquid, float, sink, rise, fall, bubbles, gas, fizzy

✓ investigate objects and materials

✓ ask and answer questions about why things happen

✓ compare what happened with what they expected to happen

✓ extend their everyday language as well as their scientific language

✓ use language to organise and clarify their ideas.

They can do this by:

✓ experiencing the bubbles of gas leaving the lemonade

✓ watching raisins rise and fall in lemonade

✓ trying to explain what they can see is happening

✓ annotating drawings of the raisins in the lemonade

✓ talking about what happens when there isn't any gas in the lemonade

✓ comparing what happens to raisins in lemonade and other liquids.

You should see evidence of their thinking and learning in:

✓ how they respond to questions

✓ how they talk about their experiences of feeling the gas leaving the lemonade

✓ the language they use to explain what happens to the raisins

✓ how well they observe and compare what happens

✓ the annotations on their drawings

✓ how they engage in the activity

✓ how much they can do without help.

Extending the activity

We put raisins in the pot. This is what we saw.

We added lemonade. This is what we saw.

Encourage the children to annotate their drawings of the raisins in lemonade. This will help them to focus on the raisins moving up and down in the liquid until all the gas is dispersed, or how closely the bubbles crowd onto each raisin before it rises up through the lemonade.

STRATEGY:

Annotated drawing

Pre-writers can have their comments scribed onto their drawings if desired.

Were there things that surprised them? Do they have more ideas to explore that might help them explain what is happening?

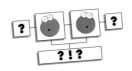

Compare and contrast

The children can compare the raisins in the bubbly lemonade and in the lemonade without bubbles.

Encourage children to look closely at the movement, or lack of movement, of raisins in water, milk, squash, soda water, cola, etc.

Does what they see confirm their ideas of why the raisins move? If not, do they need to try out other ideas to compare what happens to the raisins in the lemonade and in other situations?

You can extend this activity by comparing the raisins with other small objects that usually sink. Can they find anything else that behaves like the raisins? (Avoid peanuts.)

Creating a supportive atmosphere: Talk partners and Pair, share, square

This is a good activity to use pair, share, square to help the children come to some conclusions about what is happening to the raisins, and to raise more questions to investigate. Pairs working together are likely to explore more ideas than children working alone.

Allow the children time to watch the raisins rise and fall in the lemonade. Ask them to observe very carefully and to describe to their partner exactly what they can see happening.

Pairs can then discuss their observations and what they think is happening with another pair. All you are looking for here is a simple description of what the bubbles are doing, and how there are lots of bubbles on the raisins when they are rising, some bubbles pop, the raisins sink, etc...

MAKE ME A DUCK

12

What it is

Children use a dice game to make a given animal or object. They use different forces, such as pushes and pulls, on a modelling material to create their animal. The finished object can be compared with a photograph or a living example to see how closely they matched the real thing.

Getting started

- Make some instruction cards. For young children only use the word push and pull.

1 = push	2 = pull	3 = push
4 = pull	5 = push	6 = pull

- Older children could use a card with numbers 1 – 6, which are linked to either a push, a pull, a twist, a bend, etc. For example:

1 = push	2 = pull	3 = twist
4 = bend	5 = squeeze	
6 = You choose which force to use!		

- Collect some modelling material such as play dough and some dice, one set for each group.

 Warn children not to eat the modelling material. Children should wash hands thoroughly before and after using play dough or other modelling material.

How to use it

First of all, discuss the meaning and sensations of push and pull with the children.

Before they begin the game, give them the goal to achieve. For example, "I want you to make me a duck out of this lump of playdough. You can only push or pull. Take turns and throw the dice to find out what to do."

For each roll of the dice, they match the number with the instruction on the card. Younger children can simply use a push for each time they roll an odd number and a pull for the even numbers. Alternatively, you could stick the words push and pull on a die. Children can work in pairs or small groups.

At the end, take a little time to compare the finished products with ones from other groups. Also look at pictures of a real duck and note how their own models could be improved.

Key questions

How do you do a push or a pull?

What does a duck look like?

How is a duck different from us?

How can you use a push or a pull to make an eye/bill/tail?

What is the difference between your duck, another group's duck and real ducks?

Why not use the game to make other animals?

Looking for evidence of thinking and learning

In this activity children will have the opportunity to:

- ✓ learn that pushes and pulls are examples of forces
- ✓ learn about differences between living things
- ✓ use and explore the meaning of key vocabulary – push, pull, twist, bend, stretch, squash, longer, shorter, fatter, thinner, rounder, flatter
- ✓ be confident to initiate ideas
- ✓ take turns and work as part of a group
- ✓ learn to manipulate materials.

They can do this by:

- ✓ playing the dice game to make a duck
- ✓ considering what makes a duck – beak, feathers, 2 wings, etc
- ✓ working with a group to make a duck and comparing their duck with another group's duck and with other animals
- ✓ making an annotated drawing or photo of their duck
- ✓ comparing and contrasting animals.

You should see evidence of their thinking and learning in:

- ✓ the way that they respond to questions
- ✓ how they work with other children to play the game
- ✓ the way that they respond to the instructions
- ✓ the words about forces they use when making the duck
- ✓ what they notice when they compare and contrast animals
- ✓ the words that they use to annotate their picture
- ✓ the way that they engage in the activity
- ✓ what they can do without help.

"I need to make a beak. I hope I get a pull!"

"I've got a 5 – got to squeeze now. Can I make a duck's leg with a squeeze?"

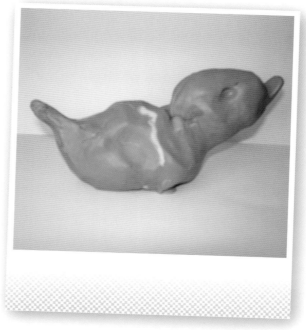

"This duck looks funny. His eyes are popping out. I'll put them back in with a push."

Extending the activity

This graphic organiser is an ideal way to get children to think more about the features of different animals. When they have finished they could play the game again but this time make the other animal.

Are there some things that they are not certain about? Does finding out using photographs, books or computers help?

Deliberate mistakes

You could introduce the activity by demonstrating how to make a creature, such as a cat, using pushes and pulls. If you deliberately make mistakes in your model, they will soon let you know … but make them explain why it's a mistake. "Tell me how you know this is not a cat?" You could also do a push when it should be a pull and so on. Are any of the children confused about pushes, pulls etc? Does playing with toys that they pull and push help?

Annotated drawing and Compare and contrast

When the model duck is completed and children have had a chance to discuss its good and not so good points, children could draw their model or take a digital photograph of it.

They could then compare their own model with a photograph/video of a real duck, consider the different parts of their duck and how well it matches the real duck. Encouraging them to jot a few notes alongside their drawing could help them develop and clarify their understanding. Are all children able to notice the differences? Does giving them some clues help them to understand?

Splat!

Display a large 3 X 3 grid, which shows the names or pictures of 9 different animals. You could try tortoise, dog, fish, frog, fly, crocodile, robin, snake and worm.

Split the class into groups and have one child from each group in front of the grid. Read out a sentence, which gives some description of one of the animals. For example, "This animal can fly." Keep giving extra bits of information until one child knows the answer and 'splats' a hand over one of the animals on the grid.

Encourage the child to explain their choice to the rest of the class. Alternatively, small tabletop grids per group or per individual can be used in the same way. Are there any animals that they are confused about? Does doing more research about the animals help?

LIQUID LAYERS

What it is

This activity encourages children to take a close look at a variety of everyday liquids and observe how they behave. Liquids are added to each other and children observe what happens. The outcomes take many children by surprise. They will look at all liquids carefully in future!

This activity can be done as a speaking and listening exercise or a simple worksheet can be used to record children's ideas. They are encouraged to think about what will happen based on their everyday experience. Tell them it's OK if they are not sure.

Getting started

- ☐ Collect a bottle of cooking oil, a can of golden syrup, water in a bottle. Find some shallow containers to put some of the liquid in.
- ☐ Collect tall, straight-sided glasses or clear plastic beakers.
- ☐ Find some food colouring plus a plastic dropper.
- ☐ A collection of small heavy and light objects may also be needed.

 If using glass, make sure any breakages are cleared away quickly. Have paper towels handy. At the end, pour the liquids into a bag for disposal, to avoid clogging sinks. Wash the remnants away using hot soapy water.

How to use it

Allow the children to observe and/or handle the oil, syrup and water. They can tip jars of the liquids backwards and forwards and observe their movement. Talk about where they might have seen each of these liquids at home or in school. Pour each one from its container into a dish, so that it can be stirred and touched.

If you are going to use a recording sheet (see Observe, predict, observe, explain, later in this section), show this to the children now.

Add the liquids in this order:

1. golden syrup 2. cooking oil 3. water 4. drops of food colouring*

Before each addition, ask the children to talk to their partner about what they think will happen and why. After the addition, ask them to describe what they saw and why they think it happened.

Smaller quantities of the liquids can be poured into small tubes so individual children can explore what happens if the order is changed. They can also be shaken.

*NB The result will vary depending on whether the food colour is added gently in drops or with force, in a 'jet'.

Key questions

What do you know about these liquids?

Where have you seen them before?

How are they the same and how are they different?

What do you think will happen if we put them all in the same glass?

Looking for evidence of thinking and learning

In this activity children will have the opportunity to:

- ✓ extend their knowledge of common liquids
- ✓ describe simple features of liquids
- ✓ use and explore the meaning of key vocabulary – liquid, float, sink, layer, flow, pour, mix
- ✓ describe similarities and differences
- ✓ observe closely using all their senses
- ✓ compare what happened with what they thought would happen.

They can do this by:

- ✓ observing closely syrup, oil and water
- ✓ predicting and then observing the outcome of mixing the liquids together by being encouraged to use a range of vocabulary to explain what they have observed e.g. pour, runny, above, mixed, floating, etc
- ✓ predicting how objects might behave when added to the three-liquid mixture.

You should see evidence of their thinking and learning in:

- ✓ how they respond to questions
- ✓ what they say and do when exploring the liquids
- ✓ how they compare each liquid
- ✓ what they say when the liquids are mixed
- ✓ how they describe how objects behave when added to the glass
- ✓ the completed observe, predict, observe, explain worksheet
- ✓ the way that they engage in the activity
- ✓ how much they can do without help.

"I think the golden syrup and oil will all mix up together."

"The water will go on top of the syrup and oil."

"Look what's happened!"

Extending the activity

Explain that they will draw on the left hand side of the sheet what they think will happen to each liquid once it is poured into the tall, straight-sided plastic container or glass.

If something different happens, they can draw it on the right hand side. Does anything surprise them? Do they want to try out any ideas to help them to explain what happened?

STRATEGY:
Observe, predict, observe, explain

O.P.O.E

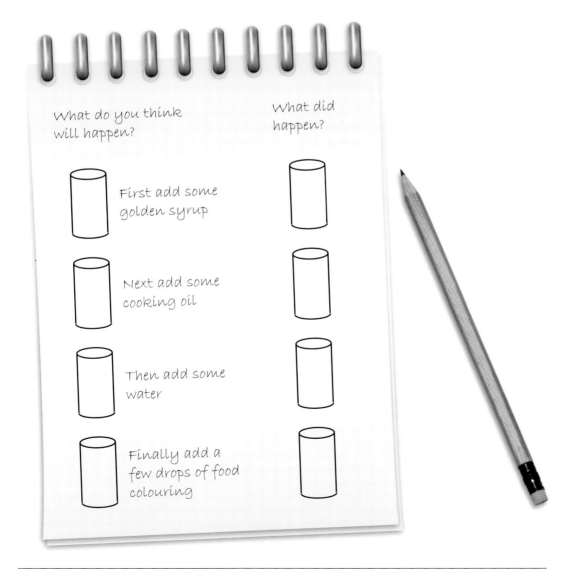

What do you think will happen?

What did happen?

First add some golden syrup

Next add some cooking oil

Then add some water

Finally add a few drops of food colouring

Observe, predict, observe, explain (version 2)

Drop a grape into water and let the children observe what happens. Ask them to talk to their partner about what will happen when you drop the grape into the glass containing the three liquids. Let them observe what happens and then try to explain in simple terms (not density) what they have seen.

Do the same with a small plastic cube. This can be in a different container if you wish but children enjoy seeing objects floating in different places in the same jar. Can the children suggest anything else that is small that might float or sink. Does trying a new object (e.g. a small marble) make it easier to predict what will happen to the next one? Does it raise any questions that they might like to explore?

NB It is best to do this activity together with the children to prevent the container becoming totally filled with sticky, greasy objects.

Creating a supportive atmosphere: No hands up, Coming to you soon and Talking thumbs

The children get excited when asked to decide what is going to happen to each liquid as it is added to the glass. This is a good activity to use strategies that keep the children thinking, but dissuade them from shouting out their ideas and unduly influencing the others. "Don't put your hands up, everyone, because when you have all done some thinking and talking I am going to choose who will tell us all about it."

If you are asking children to record their thoughts, you could use Talking thumbs to check their understanding of what they are meant to do throughout the activity. "Show me if you understand what I want you to do."

FIND ME A RAINBOW

14

What it is

By making children aware of the huge variety of colours in the environment, you can help them improve their observational skills and their understanding of the rich diversity in nature and seasonal changes. This activity helps children to search their outdoor environment for materials that will match a given colour. The less mature or experienced the child, the simpler the palette that should be used.

Getting started

- ☐ Tour your outdoor environment, check for any potential hazards and look for interesting areas to visit.
- ☐ Prepare a set of simple colour palettes for your children to use.
- ☐ Put splashes of different colours down one side of the card and a strip of double-sided tape down the adjacent side.
- ☐ Three or four colours may be enough for the youngest children.

Check the policy for working outdoors and that there are no potentially dangerous objects or harmful plants in the area. Ensure that children only collect small samples of plants. Warn them not to stick small creatures, such as ladybirds, on the palette just because they are red!

How to use it

Give pairs of children their own colour palette. You could tell them that a rainbow has fallen out of the sky and is scattered across their playground or field. It is their task to find bits of it to match the colours that they have been given.

Give children time to explore the area, talking and thinking about their colours. When they have had time to think, let them start collecting. Small samples of twigs, leaves, petals, etc can be stuck onto the double-sided tape.

Using different shades of one colour can provide an extra challenge. For example, using several shades of green will encourage children to look very closely at all the leaves in their environment and help them to recognise the range of individual colours.

It is up to you to decide if the children can add manufactured products, e.g. sweet wrappers, onto their palettes.

I have also tried this activity successfully using paint chart strips from DIY stores.

Key questions

How many of these colours do you think you can find outside?

Where do you think you will find the different colours?

Which colour do you think you will find most often?

Will the range of colours change if we go out in autumn or spring?

Looking for evidence of thinking and learning

In this activity children will have the opportunity to:

- ✓ explore and learn about the natural environment
- ✓ use and explore the meaning of key vocabulary – flowers, leaves, berries, living, dead, natural, manufactured, colour, shade
- ✓ look for similarities and differences in the natural environment, e.g. on the playing field, under the trees, etc.
- ✓ compare what they found with what they expected to find
- ✓ develop their observational skills
- ✓ expand their knowledge of colours and skills of colour matching
- ✓ recognise that there are hazards related to living things.

They can do this by:

- ✓ exploring the natural environment closely to find a range of colours
- ✓ making a list of what they think they will find
- ✓ matching objects to the particular colour on their colour palette
- ✓ comparing what they find with other children's palettes
- ✓ grouping colours together.

You should see evidence of their thinking and learning in:

- ✓ how they respond to questions
- ✓ their completed rainbow palettes
- ✓ what they say about how the plants and other materials they find match with what they thought they would find
- ✓ they way in which they compare and contrast different palettes to look for similarities and differences
- ✓ their predictions about what they think they will find outside
- ✓ the way that they engage in the activity
- ✓ how much they can do without help.

What children do and say

"The middle of this orange flower is black ... where shall I put it on my card?"

"I think I'll find lots of brown outside by the kitchen 'cos we've got lots of wooden fences and benches and doors there."

Extending the activity

COLOUR	What we think we might find	PUT THE OBJECT HERE	SENTENCE
brown	dead leaf		We found a broken brown twig.
yellow	buttercup		We found a small, yellow flower.

STRATEGY:

Making a list

Children could make lists of what they think they'll find to compare with what they actually do find. This will help you and them to think about what they already know and to refine their ideas. Are there any surprises? Does looking outside again, or asking other children what they found, help to answer any questions?

Extending the activity cont.

Classifying and grouping

Look at all the completed cards and name the things found – plants, plastics, stone, fabrics, etc. A spectrum of all the blues/greens/browns found could be created by cutting individual strips from each of the different palettes and compiling them on one sheet. How do these colour strips compare with the paint charts from paint suppliers?

Are there more of some colours than others? Why might that be? Would looking outside again on another day or at other times of the year make a difference?

Observe, predict, observe, explain

Ask children to make their own colour-matching palette. They must choose a number of colours that they think they will be able to find in the chosen environment. Afterwards the children can review what surprised them. Does what they have learnt now help them to predict what might happen if they do the same activity at another time?

Compare and contrast

Discuss the completed palettes from two different children or two different parts of the school's grounds. How are they the same and how are they different? How many different plants or other objects have been found? Which colours were easiest/ most difficult to find? Are there any surprises? Does going outside for another visit help to answer some of their questions.

Sequencing

Using the completed palettes as a 'map reference' and detailing what has been found at different points, the children could compile a sequenced description of a route around the school. Digital photographs could also be added to enrich the description. What would the same route be like next month or in a few months time?

ICE

15

GARDENS

What it is

Children collect and arrange a variety of leaves, flowers, buds, etc in a shallow tray e.g. polystyrene supermarket produce tray, ice cream container or similar. These are then frozen inside a thin layer of ice to produce beautiful Ice Gardens that attract observations, stimulate imaginations and can lead to creative outcomes in speaking and listening, art or writing.

Getting started

- ☑ Put some interesting natural objects in the bottom of a tray. Pour in a shallow layer of water (which can be coloured with food colouring) to float the objects and then place in the freezer. When it is frozen, add more water and freeze again.
- ☑ Collect more trays for the children to use.
- ☑ Find some food colouring.
- ☑ Gather together a collection of interesting natural materials or organise for children to collect their own.

 If children are to collect their own natural objects, check the policy for working outdoors and that there are not any harmful plants in the area.

How to use it

For this activity, it is a good starting point to show the children 'one that I made earlier'. This helps them to visualise what their own garden could include. Give them time to talk to each other about what they can see and how you might have made the Ice Garden.

As individuals select their samples, it is the ideal time to discuss differences and similarities between the flowers, fruit and leaves – consider colour, size, shape, number of petals, seeds, etc. Also practise counting, or graph making, by observing how many different leaves or flowers are used.

Once water is added to their tray, children will see the contents float on top of the liquid - discuss the problem of how to get the leaves and flowers inside the ice.

Place the trays in the freezer for a couple of hours and show the children the results. They may now see, if they hadn't worked it out already, that they can put a second layer of water over the contents and freeze it again.

Give children time to observe and record (through painting or drawing) the Ice Gardens as they melt.

Key questions

Look closely, what can you see?

Are all plants safe to pick?

Which of these are flowers/leaves/fruit? How do you know?

Where would you like to go to choose your samples?

Looking for evidence of thinking and learning

In this activity children will have the opportunity to:

- ✓ find out about, and identify the features of, living things
  (e.g. leaves, flowers and fruit)
- ✓ explore and describe how water is changed by cooling and explore
  freezing and melting
- ✓ use and explore the meaning of key vocabulary – float, sink, freeze,
  melt, plants, flowers, petals, leaves, fruit, berries
- ✓ observe how materials behave
- ✓ describe similarities and differences
- ✓ recognise that there are hazards related to living things.

They can do this by:

- ✓ collecting and selecting plant material and creating an Ice Garden
- ✓ observing what happens when the water is frozen
- ✓ observing the change when the ice melts
- ✓ sequencing or creating a set of instructions for making the Ice
  Garden
- ✓ grouping natural and manufactured materials.

You should see evidence of their thinking and learning in:

- ✓ how they respond to questions
- ✓ what they observe and recognise when they are collecting their
  plant material
- ✓ how they plan to make the garden with their partner
- ✓ what they say about their finished gardens and their drawings of
  the garden melting
- ✓ their sequence or instructions for making an Ice Garden
- ✓ how they sort natural and manufactured materials
- ✓ the way that they engage in the activity
- ✓ what they can do without help.

What children do and say

"When I shine the light through my Ice Garden the colours are really bright."

"My leaves are right inside the ice."

"How long will my garden take to melt?"

Extending the activity

You can create a series of pictures and words, then show the whole process of making the Ice Garden through to the point at which it melts. Ask the children to work in pairs to see if they can sort the pictures into the right sequence and then add the words to explain what is happening. Does looking at the Ice Gardens again help them to remember the sequence? How would the Pair, share, square approach help?

NB More photographs are available on the CD.

Extending the activity cont.

Create a list of instructions

Children can work in pairs to make a set of instructions for another class to follow to help them make Ice Gardens too. Do they remember to include making sure that the flowers and leaves end up in the middle of the ice? Do they remind other children to watch and record as the ice melts? Does looking at the Ice Gardens again help them to create the instructions? How would the Pair, share, square approach help?

Classifying and grouping

Make a collection of natural and manufactured materials. Tell the children that they need to decide which things can go in an Ice Garden. Remind them that only natural things can go into the garden. Give them time to work together in pairs or small groups to decide which things go in the garden and which don't. How will they find out if they are not sure? Would it help to use Phone a friend, to ask someone else what they think?

Creating a supportive atmosphere: Thinking time and Talk partners

This is an ideal opportunity to help children to build confidence in answering questions by giving them thinking time and letting them work with talk partners.

Ask the class, "Look carefully and quietly at my Ice Garden on your own. Think about what you can see. I'm going to hide it in a minute then you can talk with your partner to see how many things you can remember."

"Think on your own for a minute and then talk to your partner to decide how to make an Ice Garden like the one I showed you."

"Now you both have all your plants and leaves collected, can you tell me what your partner is planning to put in her garden?"

"Let's try putting some leaves into a water-filled tray. The leaves float to the top … how can we make sure the leaves are covered by ice? Think about these questions on your own and then have a chat with your talk partner about what you've decided."

BAGS OF FUN

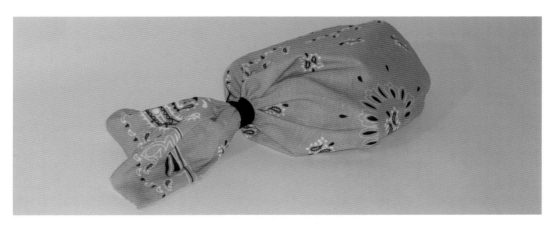

16

What it is

Several interesting items are bundled up into a large square of fabric. Children open and examine their parcel and discuss similarities and differences between the objects found inside. You may like to match the contents of your bags to your science topic e.g. Magnets, Pushes and pulls, Keeping warm, Light and dark, etc. Alternatively, you may like to use this activity solely to promote observation and discussion by including a random selection of objects.

Getting started

- ☐ Collect several squares of fabric - I find old scarves a bright and useful source for this.
- ☐ Put a selection of items into the centre of each fabric square.
- ☐ Lift all four corners to the centre and secure with a thick rubber band or a hair 'Scrunchy' (see photograph).

Stimulating items could include: old mobile phones; different (washed) fruits; little rocks and stones; stretchy things; animals made of different materials; fasteners and small bottles of liquid (shampoo, bubble bath etc) – such as those you find free in hotels.

How to use it

The best way to use these bags it to create a sense of excitement and mystery. You have found the bag and you don't know what is in it. The children are very special because they can peep inside and explore what's there. Give each group of four a bag, ask them to open it and look carefully at the items inside. They can handle the objects but they may need reminding to be careful with the liquids or any breakable items.

It is important that they are given plenty of time to explore and talk together about what is inside the bags. It is best if they are left alone for a while before you try to focus their explorations and observations by the use of questions. First they identify something that each object has in common – a similarity. Then they look for something that's different about particular items.

Try to encourage creative language and imaginative suggestions for how the items are linked. The activity can be extended by asking each group to jot down ideas that can then be passed to the next group. When the remaining groups investigate the contents, they have to try to find additional similarities and differences.

Key questions

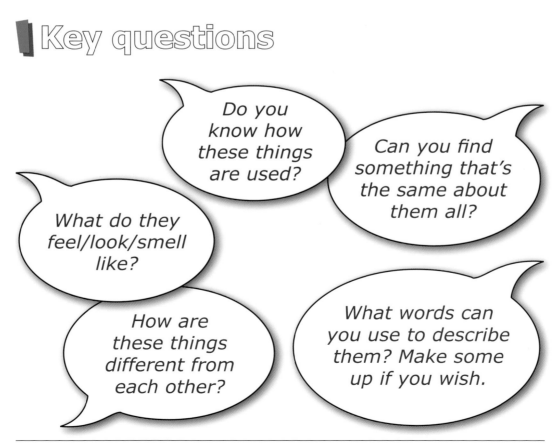

Do you know how these things are used?

Can you find something that's the same about them all?

What do they feel/look/smell like?

How are these things different from each other?

What words can you use to describe them? Make some up if you wish.

Looking for evidence of thinking and learning

In this activity children will have the opportunity to:

✓ use language to describe simple features of objects
✓ use and explore the meaning of key vocabulary – similar, different, smells, sounds, feels, see, touch, hear
✓ use their senses to explore similarities and differences
✓ make simple comparisons
✓ explain their choices
✓ use creative ideas to create an imaginative story
✓ work in groups to form a consensus.

They can do this by:

✓ exploring collections of objects in bags
✓ looking for similarities and differences and compare and contrast items
✓ identifying the odd one out
✓ creating a story that includes as many of the items as possible.

You should see evidence of their thinking and learning in:

✓ the way that they respond to questions
✓ the language that they use to describe the objects
✓ the similarities and differences that they identify and how they compare and contrast items
✓ the way they discuss ideas with classmates
✓ how they use their ideas in a story
✓ how they justify their choices or complete the odd one out activity
✓ how they engage in the activity
✓ how much they can do without help.

"These are all the same because we'd put them on a Christmas tree."

"But they're different too 'cos some of them are made of glass and some of them are wool and knitted."

"I love mobile phones!"

Extending the activity

If you choose the items carefully, you will include some that are the same but different! For example, five mobile phones but only one that flips open, or an old one that is much larger; animals with patterned coats and one plain one; several shakers that can make a loud sound but one that is fairly quiet, however hard you shake it; etc.

Children have to explain why the item is the odd one out. Be prepared for children to come up with the unexpected. This is all part of encouraging them to think creatively. If children are coming up with a limited range of ideas, would modelling an example for them help them to think more creatively about the properties of the objects in their bags?

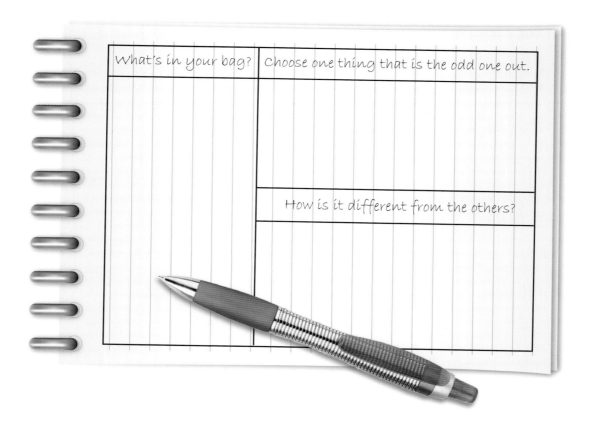

What's in your bag? | Choose one thing that is the odd one out.

How is it different from the others?

Compare and contrast

Bags that have a variety of apparently disconnected objects will provide the children with lots of opportunities to compare and contrast the material - use, weight, shape, colour, size and so on. Children group these in as many ways as they can. The odd one out challenge is even more interesting and demanding with a mixed bag of objects. Are children using a limited range of descriptive words? Does providing access to a creative word bank extend the words that they use?

Create a story

Give each pair of children one of the bags and ask them to explore the contents with care. After a few minutes, tell them that each of the objects is part of a story. Challenge the pairs to create a story, referring to as many of the items as they can in the text. Give them a limited time for this or it can take most of the day! Pairs can swap bags and create further stories if time allows. Comparing the outcomes will show a range of scenarios for each of the bags.

You could also give them sentence starters and let each pair think of how it will end using their object. They then have to add another sentence to say what happened next. Choose the starters to suit the object you have provided.

For example:
We were walking down the street when . . . . (Mum's mobile rang. She flipped the lid open, there was a shower of stars and a brightly coloured bird flew up into the air above us. . . . . .)

Just after I woke up I . . . . . (found a small spotty animal in the corner of my room. It looked at me and pointed with its front leg to a little gap in the floor. . . .)

There was a knock on the door and then . . . . . (a huge rattling and scrattling sound. I opened the door slowly to find a very small red box on the door step. . .)

Are children coming up with a limited range of ideas? Does modelling sentence completion help them? Does the Pair, share, square approach help to create new ideas?

MATERIALS SORT

17

What it is

This activity involves children sorting a range of materials – wood, plastic, metal, glass - into groups. It challenges children to consider a range of objects, identify the material that they are each made from and discuss how they can be sorted if they are made from one or more than one material.

Getting started

- ☐ Collect objects made from one material only. Choose common materials such as wood, plastic, metal, paper, glass, etc.
- ☐ Find several objects made of two or more materials.
- ☐ Hide the objects in a box or place them under a cover to keep them from view.
- ☐ Place a number of hoops on the ground. You will need the same number of hoops as the number of different materials used for making the objects.

 Check the school's policy on the use of glass. If you do use it, clear up any breakages immediately to avoid injury.

How to use it

Ask the children to find themselves a Talk (or Whisper) partner.

Tell the class that you are not going to tell them what you are doing but you want them to watch very carefully and try to work it out. Children can whisper to their partners as soon as they think they know what is happening but they cannot tell anyone else.

Start by placing a plastic object in one hoop, followed by a wooden object in a different hoop and so on. Keep doing this until you have a few items in each hoop. When you feel enough children have got the idea, try holding up an object and looking puzzled about where it should go. Have a set of large labels ready to label each hoop - PLASTIC, METAL, GLASS, WOOD etc.

Try putting an object into the wrong hoop and see if they notice. They usually gasp and shout their protests at their teacher's 'mistake'! Now hold up an object constructed of two materials such as a fork made of both wood and metal, or a plastic and metal pencil sharpener. Look puzzled or say "Oh, no! Now where can I put this?"

Children can talk to their partners to come up with a solution. If they've seen Venn diagrams, someone usually suggests that overlapping two of the hoops will solve the problem. If not, work through the problem with the children to help them to see how overlapping hoops can help.

Key questions

Can you see what I'm doing?

Why do you think I'm putting this here? ... Have a chat with your partner.

What do you notice about all of these things?

Where should this wooden spoon go?

Looking for evidence of thinking and learning

In this activity children will have the opportunity to:

✓ learn about the properties of materials and their different uses

✓ learn the names of materials

✓ use and explore the meaning of key vocabulary – types of material e.g. glass, metal, wood, plastic, properties of materials – flexible, solid, transparent

✓ talk with a classmate to clarify their ideas and solve problems

✓ create groups of objects with similar characteristics

✓ understand how a Venn diagram is useful for sorting

✓ recognise similarities and differences.

They can do this by:

✓ working with a partner to sort objects by their properties

✓ sorting objects made of more than one material

✓ using a Venn diagram to sort objects

✓ consider similarities and differences of materials while identifying the odd one out

✓ comparing and contrasting materials and creating a list of named materials.

You should see evidence of their thinking and learning in:

✓ how they respond to your questions

✓ the way they talk together and the ideas that they put forward

✓ the way they recognise and name different materials

✓ the way they sort objects using a Venn diagram

✓ the reasons that they give for the odd one out

✓ what they say when they compare and contrast the materials

✓ the items that they include in their list of objects

✓ how they engage in the activity

✓ what they can do without help.

Speech bubble: *That's easy. It's metal, so it goes in that hoop.*

Venn diagram labels: **metal**, **wood**, **metal and wood**

"This one's metal and wood. Can we put it in between the hoops?"

"I can see right through all the things made of glass."

Extending the activity

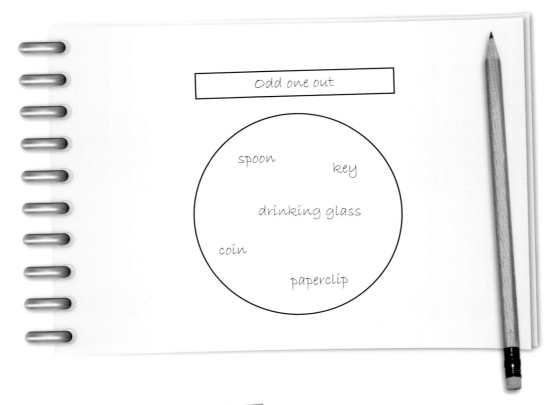

Odd one out

- spoon
- key
- drinking glass
- coin
- paperclip

STRATEGY:

Odd one out

Put a set of metal items and one made of glass into a hoop. Ask the children to talk about what you are doing. Children normally spot the odd one out speedily. Encourage them to explain why it is different. Ask groups to produce an odd one out for the rest of the class. Help children to recognise that there can be more than one reason why something is the odd one out.

Use the Pass the parcel strategy. Ask one pair to think of an item made of a material that you have chosen. They choose another pair who then do the same. When you say "Odd one out", the next pair have to come up with an object made of a different material. Are some children struggling to identify an odd one out? Will more experience of sorting and grouping items help them?

Extending the activity cont.

Making a list

Show the children a number of objects, including some made from one type of material (e.g. a coin) and some from two types (e.g. metal scissors with plastic handles). Invite the children to talk together to create a list of ten objects made from only one material. They can follow this with a list of ten objects made from two types of material. More mature children will enjoy the challenge of finding objects made from three, four or more types of material (e.g. a shoe, a reading lamp, etc).

Do some children struggle to recognise materials? Would it be useful to let them help you to construct a Materials display or let them play more sorting games?

Compare and contrast

While the children are sorting the objects by the material that they are made from, you can encourage them to compare and contrast the items and note the differences that they can see.

A simple graphic organiser could be used to compare and contrast a metal spoon and a drinking glass in terms of shininess, transparency, use, shape, etc. You can start them off by giving the children one way in which the items are different. When you have a list of differences, you can encourage the children to identify some of the ways in which the items are the same (e.g. they are both hard, they are both heavy).

Are some children uncertain of how to compare the objects? Would it help to think together to create a word bank of a wide range of characteristics of the materials?

RACING LIQUIDS

18

What it is

Children race everyday liquids down a smooth ramp and watch for differences in their movements or speed. They try to predict which will win and why. This could be linked with **Activity 2, Bubble Bubble**.

Getting started

- Collect liquids of different consistencies such as water, tomato ketchup, vegetable oil, shampoo, bubble bath, syrup, etc.
- Construct a 'race track' from a non-absorbent material such as a tray or a smooth sheet of perspex, plastic or metal. The track will need something like a brick or box to support it at one end.
- Add a thin strip of tape at the beginning and at the end of the track to act as a 'start line' and a 'finish line'.
- Collect a set of identical spoons, one for each liquid.

 Make sure that there are plenty of paper towels or sponges available to mop up spills. Warn the children not to taste any of the liquids.

How to use it

Discuss the different liquids with the children. If possible let them feel each of the liquids or pour them, or stir them as in **Activity 2, Bubble Bubble**. Give them time to talk with a partner about how the liquids feel and what they think each one is. Encourage them to share ideas.

Tell them you want to race the liquids down a hill to see which move the fastest and reach the finish line first. Give them time to talk together about what they think will happen, before the race begins! Which liquid gets to the finish line fastest? Which is second/third/fourth?

When you are ready, put a measured amount of each liquid at the start line. Then lift and tilt the tray and lean it on something like a large book or brick to create a ramp. Encourage them to talk about what happened and why (see Observe, predict, observe, explain - later in this section). If you put the liquids into the fridge for half an hour and try again it will 'thicken' some of the liquids and could produce a few surprises.

I've also done this activity by putting a teaspoon of different liquids in the bottom of large, plastic test tubes (see Resources), then asking a set of children to turn the tubes onto their flat tops at the same time and to watch what happens.

Key questions

Where have you seen these liquids before?

Do they look/ feel/move in the same way?

Which ones do you think will move slowly and which quickly?

What do you think will happen if we put them in the fridge first?

Looking for evidence of thinking and learning

In this activity children will have the opportunity to:

✓ explore and describe the observable properties of everyday liquids

✓ explore and describe how liquids change when they are cooled

✓ use and explore the meaning of key vocabulary – liquid, flow, thickness, runniness, slowest, quickest

✓ make simple comparisons

✓ group and classify everyday materials

✓ compare what happened with what they expected to happen.

They can do this by:

✓ stirring or touching a variety of common liquids

✓ predicting, observing and explaining what happens when the liquids are raced against each other

✓ comparing fast and slow liquids

✓ thinking about the behaviour of liquids by using sentence cards and/or concept mapping.

You should see evidence of their thinking and learning in:

✓ the way that they answer questions

✓ the way that they describe the thickness and speed of movement of different liquids

✓ any predictions that they make

✓ how they talk about and explain what actually happened

✓ their completed compare and contrast tables

✓ the ideas that they connect together, and why, when using sentence cards and/or concept maps

✓ the way that they engage in the activity

✓ what they can do without help.

Ooh, look how quick that one is!

The others have only just started to run. They are slower.

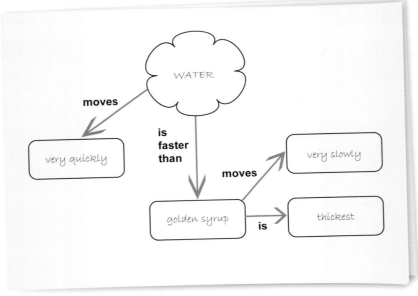

Extending the activity

At the end of the activity the children can review their findings and complete a simple table to put the liquids into order by speed. Then they can also look at thickness, stickiness, colour, etc. They may see a pattern developing. They might say, "The golden syrup was slowest." ... however, that does not tell us anything about patterns. You could ask, "Why do you think that is? In what ways is golden syrup like the other liquids that went slowly down the ramp?"

Sort the liquids into the ones that were fast and the ones that were slow

Fast liquids	Slow liquids
fastest	
	slowest

Fast liquids get down the ramp quickly because...

You can tell a liquid is going to be slow if...

Observe, predict, observe, explain

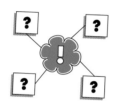

This will give children the opportunity to think more systematically about what is happening and encourage them to justify their ideas. Let them observe each liquid. Ask them to predict what will happen when the liquids are raced. Let them think on their own and then share their ideas with a talk partner. Now race the liquids and ask the children to look carefully at what is happening

Finally ask them to talk to their partner about what happened. Was it what they expected and why? Then share ideas. Can they now put the four liquids in order across the slope, so they go from fastest to slowest when they are raced?

Concept map

You could use concept mapping to produce a visual representation of what has been discovered. First decide if you'll do this with all your class or just the children who are most confident with written language.

Create large cards with appropriate words or phrases. These can be moved around to connect ideas, such as, 'golden syrup moves very slowly.' Does sharing ideas with another pair help them to clarify their ideas?

Sentence cards

Ask the children to reorganise the cards to make sensible sentences. You can make this as easy or as difficult as is appropriate for your children. Are all children able to apply their earlier experiences to sort the sentences? Would more exploration of the liquids, or someone to read the cards, help them?

The golden syrup	was as fast as the bubble bath.
The water	hardly moved at all.
Washing up liquid	moved very slowly.
Tomato ketchup from the fridge	ran fastest down the slope.

QUICKDRAW 19

What it is

This is a simple drawing activity that encourages good listening and good description and provokes lots of specific questioning.

The activity can be done in small groups, pairs or even with the whole class. Children need to either describe carefully or to listen, question and then draw carefully. The idea is to listen to the information from someone describing a picture, to question if necessary and then to draw carefully.

Getting started

- ▣ Collect a set of photographs. Each one needs to show a clear, simple image of an animal. If possible, include birds, reptiles, minibeasts, fish, amphibians as well as the more common mammals.
- ▣ Each child needs paper and a pencil or pencil crayons. Choose drawing materials that allow them to make fine lines.
- ▣ Organise the children so that those drawing cannot see the images being described.

How to use it

One child is allowed to see the photograph. This child names and describes the animal to their partner, or the rest of the group, who cannot see the image. The children doing the drawing can ask questions to help to clarify what it looks like.

Children tend to dive into the drawing, before they have a clear idea of whether they are drawing, for example, the whole animal or just part of the animal, the front view or the side view, stationary or moving, etc.

You might like to do a practice activity first with the whole class to demonstrate the importance of good, clear descriptions. At this point, you can also guide them into using good listening and questioning skills.

When they finish they can share their drawings and talk about how they might be improved. Did they ask the right questions?

Key questions

Do you know what kind of animal you are drawing?

Which questions could you ask to find out if you only need to draw the head of the animal?

What question could you ask if you're not sure of the shape of a part of its body?

Which questions do you need to ask to make sure you have drawn it the right way round?

Looking for evidence of thinking and learning

In this activity children will have the opportunity to:

✓ find out about, and identify, some features of living things

✓ understand the functions of visible features of animals

✓ use and explore the meaning of key vocabulary – body parts e.g. head, wings, etc; size and position e.g. bigger than, above, facing

✓ develop their listening skills

✓ use language to clarify thinking

✓ ask questions

✓ use drawing to record their understanding.

They can do this by:

✓ listening to a description of an animal and drawing the animal

✓ asking questions to help to make the drawings more accurate

✓ comparing what they have drawn with the photograph and their classmate's drawings

✓ completing a graphic organiser to think about the functions of parts of animals' bodies

✓ collecting ideas on a thinking mat.

You should see evidence of their thinking and learning in:

✓ the way that they answer questions

✓ the questions that they ask to try to make their drawing accurate

✓ their completed drawings

✓ the way that they talk about their drawings

✓ their use of descriptive language

✓ their completed graphic organiser or thinking mat

✓ the way that they respond to the activity

✓ what they can do without help.

"Which way is it looking?"

"How many eyes does it have?"

"Is it an adult or a baby?"

"What are the feet like?"

"What shape is its beak?"

"Does it lay eggs?"

"Does it have feathers showing?"

"Does it have wings?"

Extending the activity

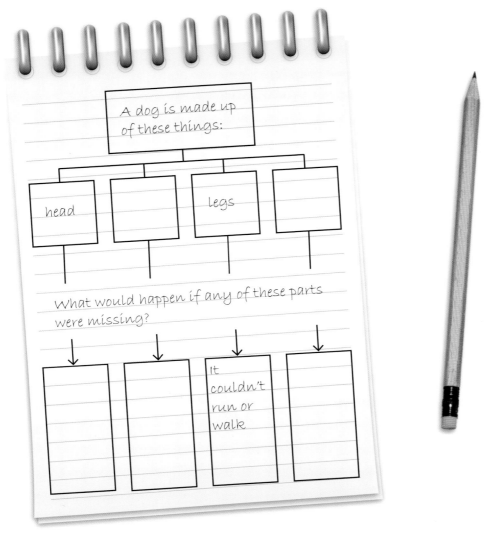

A dog is made up of these things:

head   legs

What would happen if any of these parts were missing?

It couldn't run or walk

STRATEGY:
Whole-parts graphic organiser

Using a prepared, simple graphic organiser, children can consider the importance of some major parts of an animal's body and the consequences for the animal if that part was missing. Are all children confident of the importance of each part? How would doing more research using books or the internet help?

Compare and contrast

Using a graphic organiser will enable them to compare different animals from the point of view of how they look, how they move, what they eat, where they live etc.

Are children uncertain about some of these aspects of the animals? Would access to books and the internet help them to add more detail to their graphic organiser?

Hot seating

A continuation of this activity could be that one child takes a photograph of a particular animal. The rest of the class ask questions – perhaps up to 20 – to determine which animal has been chosen.

Alternatively, with more mature children, you can put the class into groups. Each group must create a list of 'excellent questions' to see how quickly their group can discover the answer - for example, "How many legs does it have?", "Is it covered in feathers?", "Where does it live?". Are children struggling to think of questions? Would looking at a selection of animals help them? How about modelling the process first?

Thinking mats

This activity could be used to develop the children's understanding of what animals need to live healthily. (See instructions for thinking mats from the introduction.) Children can jot their ideas on their own sheet of paper or wipe board, either in words or pictures, before sharing what they think. How would the Pair, share, square approach help them to develop their ideas?

Creating a supportive atmosphere: Peer assessment

This activity is an ideal opportunity to see how well peer assessment and feedback can work if handled sensitively. Using the 'One star and a wish' strategy, learners can review each other's drawings and describe something very good about the sketch and something that could be developed.

MISSING WATER

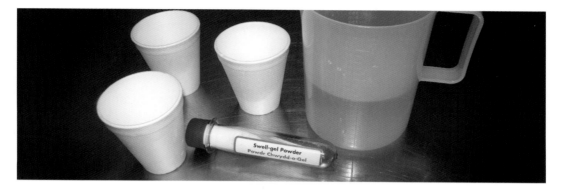

20

What it is

The children see you pour a stream of water into a cup, but it isn't there when you tip it upside down! Water retaining granules in the bottom of the cup rapidly absorb large amounts of water. Children are challenged to work out where the water has gone. Connections to everyday materials and water absorption can be explored.

Getting started

- ☐ Collect white, polystyrene cups - three for you and more for the children to do their own explorations.
- ☐ Put a small amount of water retaining granules (e.g. Swell Gel), into the bottom of one cup. Have enough water ready to fill the granules or a few 'snowflakes' fall too! Practice the activity to get a feel for the quantities needed.
- ☐ Gather items that children might suggest will retain water, e.g. powders - flour, sugar, talcum powder, etc – and tissues, paper towels, cloths and sponges, disposable nappies, towelling, etc.
- ☐ Provide bowls to avoid water spilling everywhere.

Garden centres sell water retaining granules. Read the instructions on the packet. It should say non-hazardous. However, avoid getting it into your (or a child's) eyes and mouth. If this happens, flush with large amounts of water. It is safer to do the first part of the activity as a demonstration.

How to use it

Show the children the cups ... "I have three empty white cups here." As the powder is white it is 'invisible' to the eye. Pour water into the cup with the water retaining granules and ask the children to watch this cup carefully. Move the cups around a few times (like a magician) and then ask them to point out the cup with the water. They will do this easily!

Make a show of tipping each cup upside down in turn ..."Look no water in here." Finish up with the final cup and say, "So it must be in here!" ... as you turn the cup over, the children will expect the water to pour out and they'll be amazed when it doesn't!

Now ask them to discuss with their talk partner where the water might have gone. Explore any ideas they come up with where possible.

This activity can lead to various explorations (see follow-up later in this section). Eventually you can show them the jelly-like substance inside the cup and demonstrate, by squeezing the material, how soft and squashy it is. (Wash your hands carefully afterwards.) You can also do it in a transparent container so that they can see what happens.

Key questions

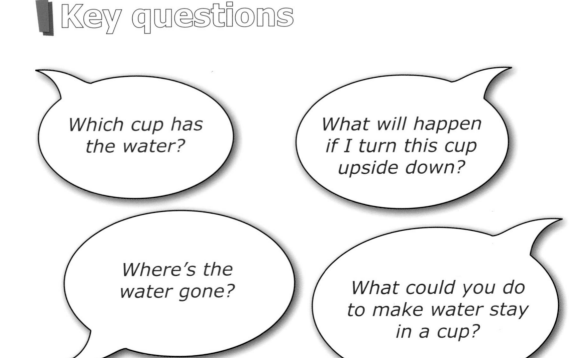

Which cup has the water?

What will happen if I turn this cup upside down?

Where's the water gone?

What could you do to make water stay in a cup?

Looking for evidence of thinking and learning

In this activity children will have the opportunity to:

✓ learn about the nature of materials and their everyday uses
✓ use and explore the meaning of key vocabulary – water, liquid, absorb, moisture, material, retaining, granules
✓ discuss a problem with a partner or a group to clarify thinking
✓ ask questions and decide how they might find answers
✓ use first-hand experience and information sources to find answers
✓ make simple comparisons.

They can do this by:

✓ watching water being poured into a cup and discussing why it seems to have disappeared
✓ trying out ideas to stop water coming out of a cup
✓ exploring absorption by comparing and contrasting different materials in terms of their absorbency
✓ using a KWHL grid to help to find out how absorbency is used in everyday lives.

You should see evidence of their thinking and learning in:

✓ the way they respond to questions
✓ the way that they explain and explore possible reasons for what they have observed
✓ how they talk about or complete the compare and contrast table
✓ the way they investigate and find out about absorbency and how they complete or talk about their KWHL grid
✓ the way that they engage in the activity
✓ what they can do without help.

Extending the activity

Young children will enjoy exploring a range of different materials that they think might give the same effect as the water retaining granules. They should be able to make their own suggestions. You may want to provide a few hints for what to try, such as flour, white sugar, salt, sand or bits of tissue. If you provide too many things, children will find it difficult to think any further.

Teacher: "Try out some of the materials that we have here. Add just a little water. Wait for a minute, then tip your cup upside down over the tray. What happens? Show me by telling, drawing or writing. What else can you think of to try?"

STRATEGY:

Compare and contrast

Be aware that some children are sensitive to soap powder – avoid, or use mild powders.

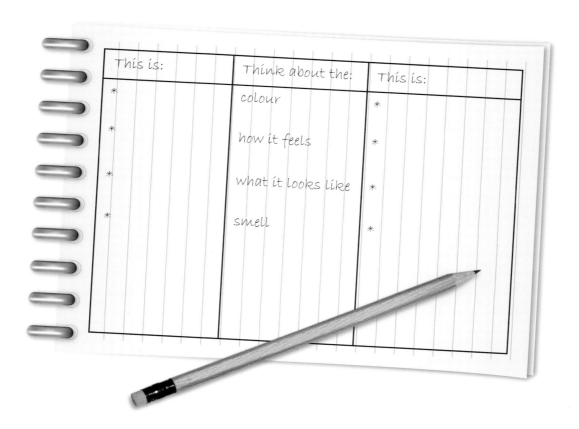

This is:	Think about the:	This is:
*	colour	*
*	how it feels	*
*	what it looks like	*
*	smell	*

KWHL grid

Show children how much water a disposable nappy can absorb. Have a row of plastic cups full of water and ask them to estimate how many you'll be able to pour into the nappy before the water starts to leak. If you do this gradually over a period of half an hour or so, the nappy may absorb even more water. Disposable nappies use water retaining materials inside. Some are similar to the granules used to hold water in plant containers. This can lead into a more general exploration and research about nappies and other absorbent materials.

An example of a KWHL grid is provided as a starting point below. Children should be encouraged to add their own ideas in writing or through discussion, using an adult as a scribe.

What we think we know	What we want to know	How we will find out	What we found out

Disposable nappies vary in how much they are able to biodegrade. Finding out more about disposable and reusable nappies could be an interesting challenge for more mature children.

Deliberate mistake

After the children have tried adding water to a variety of different materials (see Compare and contrast), tell them that, unfortunately, you've muddled up all of their results. They need to help you sort them out.

Read out sentences such as, "When we added water to the white sugar, the water turned white." "When we added water to the flour we ended up with a clear pink liquid." Most of them should notice these deliberate mistakes!

SUMMER SNOW

21

What it is

Children observe 'Magic Snow'. This is a powder that expands on contact with water. It looks a lot like snow, but it's nowhere near as cold. However, if you put it in a freezer for a short time it can be as cold as snow!

This activity allows you to become a magician! Children can explore how materials behave in unexpected ways. It links well to **Activity 20, Missing Water**, and can lead to exploring hot and cold.

Getting started

- Get some Magic Snow (see Resources). It can be dried and used again. Have water and transparent plastic containers available.
- Depending on your chosen follow-up you may need ice, ice-cream or ice-cream ingredients, crushed ice and/or materials for making play dough, gloop and slime (see Resources).

Read the instructions on the packet. Magic Snow is non-hazardous, but avoid getting any into eyes and mouth. If this happens, flush with large amounts of water.

Some children may not have experienced snow, or realise that it is very cold. Pictures of snowy places will contextualise this activity.

How to use it

Put a tablespoon of Magic Snow into a transparent, plastic container. "What do you think might happen if I add water?" Ask them to discuss in pairs or small groups. If they have seen water retaining granules in **Activity 20, Missing Water**, they may assume it will absorb water. Some children sense something unusual is going to occur and predict pops and bangs!

Have another container with 12 tablespoons of water nearby. Wave a magic wand and say a few lines of a Magic Snow Spell, such as:

Here's the dry (shake the powder) *and here's the wet* (stir the water),
Wait to see just what we'll get.
When I wave my wand about (wave your wand and mix them)
Magic snow comes tumbling out!

Children tend to be very excited at first and giggle with their friends. It may need to be repeated for them to observe calmly. Stress that you need them to observe closely, so that they can draw exactly what they see.

Give children plenty of time to talk about and explore making the 'snow'. Compare the 'snow' with the real thing if it is snowing, or other cold materials such as crushed ice and ice-cream. Challenge them to think about how they can make the 'magic snow' as cold as real snow. You could also let them experience making ice cream (see Resources).

Key questions

What does it look like?

What does it feel like?

What happens when they are mixed together?

What do the Magic Snow and water look like at the beginning?

Looking for evidence of thinking and learning

In this activity children will have the opportunity to:

✓ learn that materials can change and behave in surprising ways

✓ explore the properties of materials used in everyday life

✓ use and explore the meaning of key vocabulary – material, liquid, water, unexpected, similar to, different from, properties of materials e.g. stretchy, cold, expand

✓ observe carefully and look for similarities and differences

✓ use talk to clarify their thinking.

They can do this by:

✓ discussing what happens when water is added to Magic Snow

✓ drawing what they have seen and annotating their drawing

✓ discussing and investigating 'The Snowman's Coat' Concept Cartoon

✓ comparing Magic Snow with ice, snow and ice cream

✓ comparing Magic Snow with other unusual materials.

You should see evidence of their thinking and learning in:

✓ how they respond to questions

✓ the language they use to describe their observations and experiences

✓ what they notice about how things change

✓ the questions that they raise using the Concept Cartoon and how they investigate their ideas

✓ how they describe materials

✓ the way that they talk about or annotate their drawings

✓ a completed compare and contrast graphic organiser

✓ they way that they engage in the activity

✓ what they can do without help.

What children do and say

Wooo! It's getting bigger and bigger!

It's like a snow mountain in Austria.

It's coming out of the top and onto the table! It's not going to stop!

Extending the activity

Using a Concept Cartoon, for example 'The Snowman's Coat' (Naylor and Naylor, 2000), will encourage children to think about scientific problems, carry out an investigation and find out the answers themselves. When they have investigated the problem, are there any more questions to answer?

Extending the activity cont.

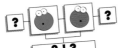

Compare and contrast

As well as comparing Magic Snow to real snow and other cold substances, you could also compare and contrast it with other unusual materials such as gloop, slime and playdough. There are recipes for these in the Resources section. Children could think about colour, stretchiness, smell, feel, texture, stickiness, etc. Alternatively, you could compare it with things that change in a surprising way, such as popcorn. Use a see-through pan to watch the popcorn explode.

Would using a simple graphic organiser help them to organise their ideas? How about providing some key ideas on word cards for children with more limited vocabulary?

Annotated drawing

If the children observe what is happening very carefully, they may be able to draw a set of pictures to show what happens as water is added to the Magic Snow. Simple annotations can be added. This leads to lots of talk as they try to explain what they saw.

If children have limited written or spoken vocabulary, you can work with them or provide key phrases to help them share their ideas.

Splat!

Display a large, 3 X 3 grid, which shows the names or pictures of 9 different materials. You could try white sugar, brown sugar, white flour, sand, Magic Snow, ice cream, icing sugar, caster sugar, ice … Split the class into groups and have one child from each group in front of the grid.

Read out a sentence, which gives some description of one of the materials. For example, "This material feels gritty. It tastes sweet. When I put it in water it turns the water brown." Keep giving extra bits of information until one child knows the answer and 'splats' a hand over one of the materials on the grid. Encourage the child to explain their choice to the rest of the class.

Alternatively, small tabletop grids can be used in the same way.

WHERE IS BENNY?

22

What it is

A familiar soft toy or puppet, chosen by the children, such as Benny shown above, is photographed in various parts of the school and its grounds. The children study the photographs to decide where their toy has been.

This activity helps to improve the children's observational skills and their geographical skills too.

Getting started

- ☐ Collect a range of soft toys, such as Benny (See Resources) and ask the children to choose one to play a special game.
- ☐ Take a series of photographs of the toy in different parts of the classroom, school building and school grounds. Don't let the children see you taking the photos.
- ☐ Laminate the photos, or scan them if you want to use them with the whole class using a whiteboard.

 Check for possible safety hazards in the places where you take the photos, since the children may go there to look for the toy. Check the school's policy for working outdoors.

How to use it

Share the photos of the toy with the children and ask them to try to decide where the photo was taken. You might give the photos to a small group or pairs of children to talk about independently first and then share each group's ideas. Alternatively, you might decide to work together with a group or the whole class.

Try to make the photos a bit challenging. For example, a teacher at Benny's school photographed him sitting near some computers. The only way that the children could tell where he was sitting was by looking very closely at what was behind him in the photo.

Another school placed their favourite teddy near the car wheels of different members of staff. The children had to investigate wheels and hubcaps before they could attempt to identify which car it was.

Key questions

How can you tell where Benny has been this week?

How can you tell which room this is?

What's behind Benny in the photograph?

What helped you to decide where he is?

Does more than one place look like this?

Has anything changed since the photo was taken?

Looking for evidence of thinking and learning

In this activity children will have the opportunity to:

- ✓ identify features of everyday objects
- ✓ look for similarities and differences
- ✓ observe closely
- ✓ discuss a problem
- ✓ make simple predictions
- ✓ explain why they have made the predictions
- ✓ use a simple map or plan.

They can do this by:

- ✓ looking closely at a set of photographs of a favourite toy in various places around the school
- ✓ talking about what they can see in the photographs
- ✓ predicting where the toy is located
- ✓ looking for evidence to see if they were right about the toy's location
- ✓ putting the photos in a sequence using a simple map or plan.

You should see evidence of their thinking and learning in:

- ✓ the way that they respond to questions
- ✓ the way that they talk about the details in the photos
- ✓ the words they use to describe and/or explain where they think the toy is
- ✓ the way that they put the pictures in a sequence
- ✓ how they use the map or plan to work out the toy's journey
- ✓ how they engage in the activity
- ✓ how much they can do without help.

What children do and say

*"He's in the garden! Look, there is a
Sunflower plant!"*

*"I think he is in the assembly hall, I can see the
climbing frame."*

Extending the activity

Tell the children that the toy has been on a journey around the school. For example, out of the classroom, across the hall, into the foyer, to the office and through the cloakroom. Take photos of key places on the journey (see the following page). Ask pairs of children to put the photos in the correct sequence. They could use a simple plan to help them.

Can all the children see the connection between the school and the plan? Does walking round the school with the plan help?

If they do this confidently then you can give them a map or plan and photos of a place that they do not know (see CD).

A related activity is to collect photographs of familiar sights round the school and cut them in half. Ask the children where it is. You will be amazed at how many times they can pass a door or window and not really notice it. Then ask the children to complete the image by drawing the other half.

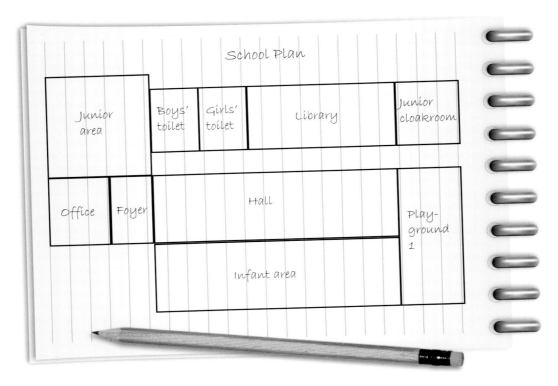

Extending the activity cont.

These photos can be used to generate discussion about where Benny has been. See also resources on the CD.

SUGARS

23

What it is

This seems like a very simple activity. It's just dissolving sugar in water. Most young children will have seen sugar dissolving in water. However, at this age, if asked what has happened to the sugar, they often say that it's 'disappeared'.

This activity encourages the children to look carefully at different types of sugar before and after they are dissolved in water. They will see a variety of results, from clear, colourless solutions to dark brown. Their explorations lead to investigations about what affects the way sugar dissolves.

Getting started

- ☐ Collect a variety of sugars, such as white granulated, icing sugar, caster sugar, dark muscovado, demerara, molasses, light brown soft sugar, coloured sugar crystals, etc.
- ☐ Get some clear, colourless, plastic or glass containers.
- ☐ Collect some spoons.
- ☐ You may want to cover the tables to avoid them getting sticky.

 Stress that children should not normally taste things in science. In this case, if you use clean containers and clean water, you could let the children taste the solutions.

If you are using glass make sure that breakages are cleared away immediately to avoid accidents.

How to use it

Invite the children to explore the different types of sugar. Encourage them to discuss with a talk partner how the sugars are similar or different. Ask them to talk to their partner about what they already know about sugar and where they have seen it used. You could collect their ideas in the first column of a KWHL grid for use at a later stage.

Tell them you are going to put some sugar into water. Some children may already be able to suggest what might happen. Give them a minute to talk to their partner about this.

Dissolve a tablespoon of granulated white sugar in some water and ask them to observe very carefully what happens. Can they explain to their partner what they have seen? If they say that it's disappeared, ask them to consider that carefully. "Where could it have gone?" "How can we tell if it's still in the water or if it has really gone completely?"

Dissolve another sugar in some water, then compare the different solutions. After watching one or two, they should be in a better position to predict what is going to happen when other sugars are added.

Give children an opportunity to explore dissolving the sugars themselves and gather together any ideas they have on a Thinking mat.

Key questions

What might happen when I put some sugar into some water?

What has happened?

How can we test to see if the sugar is still in the water?

What do you think will happen to the other sugars in water?

Looking for evidence of thinking and learning

In this activity children will have the opportunity to:

- ✓ learn that some things dissolve in water
- ✓ use and explore the meaning of key vocabulary – liquid, water, sugar, stir, dissolve, colourless
- ✓ observe how materials dissolve in water
- ✓ describe similarities and differences
- ✓ sort materials into groups based on simple properties
- ✓ use talk to explain their observations and clarify their ideas
- ✓ compare what happened with what they expected to happen
- ✓ raise simple questions and investigate their ideas.

They can do this by:

- ✓ observing what happens when sugar is added to water
- ✓ exploring, classifying and grouping different sugars
- ✓ exploring their ideas by completing concept sentences about sugars
- ✓ using a KWHL grid and/or Concept Cartoon to help them to raise questions about sugar and investigate their ideas.

You should see evidence of their thinking and learning in:

- ✓ how they respond to questions
- ✓ the language they use to describe their observations
- ✓ how they explain why different sugars produce different solutions
- ✓ how they group the different sugars
- ✓ the questions that they raise with the KWHL grid or Concept Cartoon and how they investigate their ideas
- ✓ the concept sentences that they produce
- ✓ the way that they engage in the activities
- ✓ what they can do without help.

"This icing sugar is really soft and smooth."

"The sugar is disappearing."

"These two look the same but they're different colours."

Extending the activity

Put samples of different sugars into small dishes so children can observe them closely.

"Look at all of these sugars. Find out what happens when you put them in some water. See if you can use what happens to sort them into groups. Can you tell me how you've decided to sort them?"

The children might think about crystal size, colour of the crystal, colour of the solution, taste, and so on. Do not worry about fair testing at this stage. It is good for children initially to explore their ideas without being too systematic about it. (See also Concept Cartoon on the next page.)

Note that if you use sugar cubes, the children will probably think of these as large crystals. Really they are a collection of granulated sugar crystals.

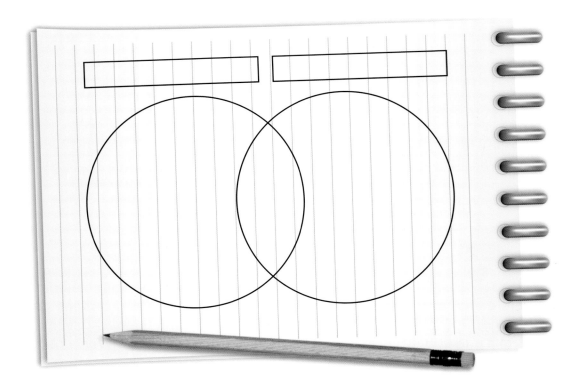

Concept sentence

Mature children should be able to make sentences out of key words that are jumbled up. Think about using words like these:

> white sugar, brown sugar, dissolves, sugar, stir,
> water, no, colour, only, always, brown, will.

This could produce sentences like:

> 'When I stir white sugar in water it has no colour.'
> 'When I stir brown sugar in water it is brown.'

KWHL grid

If you have gathered children's ideas about sugar earlier, then using a KWHL grid to explore their ideas more systematically can be helpful. There are several factors to investigate such as temperature of the water, quantity of sugar, stirring, etc. Here is an example of a KWHL grid to get the children started.

What we think we KNOW about sugar	What we WANT to find out about sugar	HOW we will find out	What we LEARNT about sugar
People use sugar to make their tea sweet.	What happens if you don't stir sugar?	Put sugar in two containers of warm water. Stir one and leave one not stirred	

Are children able to raise questions and decide how to find out? How much adult support do they need? Were there any surprises from their research and investigations? Are there new questions to answer?

Concept Cartoon™

Use the 'Time for Tea' Concept Cartoon (Naylor and Naylor, 2000). This will encourage your children to talk about how to investigate dissolving, think about problems and questions, and find out answers themselves. It will help children to work more systematically and investigate their own ideas. Were there any surprises from their investigations? Are there new questions to answer?

PAPER CLIP SPINNERS

24

What it is

This is a simple activity that involves spinning a paper clip to select from different choices of materials and objects. The children think about the relationship between the object and the material and decide if the object could realistically be made out of that material.

Children enjoy it enormously. It encourages them to think, to make decisions and to explain those decisions to others.

Getting started

- ▫ Cut two circles about 20 cm across from thin card or draw the circles on sheets of paper. Different colours are helpful. Divide each circle into 6 or 8 segments.
- ▫ Write the names of household objects (e.g. table) in one set of segments. You could add pictures as well.
- ▫ Write the names of materials (e.g. sponge, paper, etc) in the other set of segments.
- ▫ Collect a pencil and paper clip for each pair or group.
- ▫ If children are working independently, write 'Sensible', 'Not sensible' and 'Why?' on cards.

How to use it

Children use the pencil point to hold a paper clip at the centre of the 'Objects' card circle.

They spin the paper clip so that when it comes to rest it points to one of the objects. For example it might land on 'pan'.

Then they spin a paper clip on the 'Materials' circle, so that when it comes to rest it points to a material such as 'paper'.

Now the children have to decide together whether it would be sensible to make the object from that particular material.

You can ask "Is it sensible to make a pan from paper? Why do you think that?" Alternatively, the children can use 'sensible', and 'not sensible' cards to make their own decisions.

The question can take different forms, such as "Could we make windows out of rubber?" or "Would it be sensible to use wood for Wellingtons?"

Key questions

How do you think we can spin the paper clip?

Are these two things a sensible match?

Why do you think that?

What would happen if we made that object from that material?

Are there better materials that we could use?

How would you use that material?

Looking for evidence of thinking and learning

In this activity children will have the opportunity to:

✓ learn about the uses of materials and their properties

✓ learn the names of everyday objects and the materials that are used to make them

✓ use and explore the meaning of key vocabulary – material, names of materials e.g. wood, metal

✓ describe simple features of objects

✓ talk about ideas and listen to each other's ideas

✓ make decisions

✓ explain their decisions to others.

They can do this by:

✓ using spinners to match objects and everyday materials

✓ talking to others about the match between objects and materials

✓ linking objects and materials in a yes/no/maybe so game

✓ exploring objects and materials by making a list or spotting deliberate mistakes.

You should see evidence of their thinking and learning in:

✓ how they respond to questions

✓ what they say about the matches in their Paper clip spinner game

✓ the materials they suggest for different objects

✓ their responses during the yes/no/maybe so class activity and how they explain their responses

✓ the lists that they make

✓ how well they can spot deliberate mistakes

✓ how they engage in the activity

✓ how much they can do without help.

Extending the activity

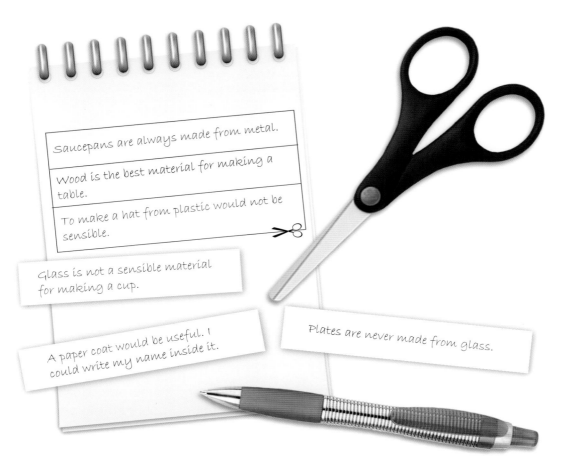

Saucepans are always made from metal.

Wood is the best material for making a table.

To make a hat from plastic would not be sensible.

Glass is not a sensible material for making a cup.

A paper coat would be useful. I could write my name inside it.

Plates are never made from glass.

STRATEGY:

Yes – no – maybe so

YES NO MAYBE

The matches from the Paper clip spinners activity can be used for playing a Yes/no/maybe so game. This is another way of getting them to explain their ideas. The 'maybe so' category allows thinking space when they need it. More mature learners might be able to make up a true/false game for other learners.

"Thumbs up if what I say is true. Thumbs down if it is not true. Thumbs sideways if you are not sure. Explain why the sentence is true or false." Are there some statements that some children are not sure about? Would giving them more time to explore materials and/or objects help?

Extending the activity cont.

You can use a much wider range of situations than objects and materials, for example:
- animals and their habitats
- animals and the foods that they eat
- clothing and different types of weather
- and so on.

Making a list

In making a list, children can go beyond a single judgement and make a series of related judgements. For example, they could make a list of:
- objects and silly materials
- all the things that metals can be used for
- all the things they know that sink
- the set of clothes that we could wear when it's raining
- all the animals that might live in a particular habitat
- and so on.

The list will help them to extend their ideas and raise questions that can lead to further enquiry. How would Pair, share, square help them to extend their ideas? What additional research or exploration can they do to extend their lists?

Deliberate mistakes

During the demonstration of this activity, try adding a few deliberate mistakes. For example, "Glass would be perfect for a hat, so I could see through it while I am walking along."

If children don't challenge this statement, ask if they could see any disadvantages to wearing a glass hat.

Moving from describing to explaining

This is a natural follow on from the Paper clip spinners activity. Their initial response is to make a judgement about how well the things match. "Why do you think that?" moves them gently and naturally towards explaining and justifying their thinking.

FEELY FEET

25

What it is

This activity focuses on what the world feels like through your feet. The experience often surprises children (and adults), since feeling with your feet can produce very different sensations from feeling with your hands. The activity could, of course, be done using hands rather than feet ... but this way is so much more fun!

Getting started

- Collect some small washing up bowls.
- Gather some interestingly textured materials such as: cotton wool, pan scourers, sand, marshmallows, glass beads, polystyrene chips, pasta (lightly cooked or uncooked), rice, breakfast cereal, sponge, scrunched up paper, cold ice packs. Let your imagination run wild.
- Fill washing up bowls with different materials. Keep the contents hidden so that it is a surprise, or you can use blindfolds.

 Get children to wash their feet first. Ensure that there are no sharp objects in the bowls. Discourage children from eating any 'food' that is used. Dispose of food after use. Make sure that the blindfolds are clean. To avoid falls due to slippery samples children could sit on a chair.

How to use it

Remind children that they normally experience how something feels with their hands. Then tell them that you want them to feel something by using their feet. Ask a volunteer to close their eyes and step into one of the bowls with bare feet. Keep the bowl hidden behind something. After a little stomping about, they can describe to everyone what it feels like and then they all try to guess what's in the bowl. Other children can do the same with different bowls.

Try out several of the materials and then extend the activity by letting all the children try all of the bowls and talk about the contents. Let them touch the contents with their hands. How different does it feel?

After this or some time later, the children can try the bowls again and try to work out what is in the bowl based on what they have experienced previously. Does that make it easier?

Encourage children to include sounds and made up words, for example, 'screeble', 'slooshy', 'crinch', 'crunch'. Share the words and sounds that children create. Work with a small group so there is plenty of opportunity to try out each material and to talk about the experience. Older or more mature children could work with a partner and record their responses on paper or a tape recorder.

Key questions

Does it feel different when you touch it with your hands or with your feet?

Do any of them feel the same?

Which ones feel soft/ smooth?

Does it remind you of anything?

Looking for evidence of thinking and learning

In this activity children will have the opportunity to:

✓ learn how the sense of touch helps us to understand the world

✓ describe simple features of materials

✓ use and explore key vocabulary – touch, feel, sensation, descriptive words e.g. smooth, soft, velvety, stiff

✓ use touch to explore and recognise similarities and differences between materials

✓ explore and experiment with words and sounds

✓ use language to imagine or recreate experiences.

They can do this by:

✓ using their feet to feel a selection of materials placed in bowls

✓ talking to their classmates about what they feel

✓ classifying and grouping using the differences between materials

✓ creating concept sentences

✓ using imaginative vocabulary and images to create a story or annotated drawing linked to what they have experienced.

You should see evidence of their thinking and learning in:

✓ the way they respond to questions

✓ the language that they use

✓ how confident they are in sharing their ideas

✓ how they apply their experience in a story or in sorting the materials

✓ how they annotate their drawings

✓ the way that they engage in the activity

✓ how much they can do without help.

Extending the activity

Give children a set of word cards. Ask them to make sentences about the materials they felt with their feet. If children are finding this demanding, will Pair, share, square or adult support help? Do children need more experience of the materials to be able to make the connections?

STRATEGY:
Concept sentences

sawdust

scourers

smooth

cotton wool

squishy

are

polystyrene

rough

plastic

corn flakes

soft

soap

glass beads

sometimes

always

warm

icy

like

similar

different

not

slippery

scratchy

is

Creating a story

You could create a story along the lines of 'We're Going on a Bear Hunt' (Rosen and Oxenbury, 1993). When children have finished exploring, encourage them to use describing words for each material, such as hard, crunchy, slippery, and travel through an imaginary journey. Turn the journey into movement, with children walking round the room, changing the way that they walk and making the sounds as they have an imaginary encounter with each material.

Are all children contributing equally to this activity? Would modelling the process help? Could a more mature pair of children work with a less confident pair as partners on the journey?

Classifying and grouping

When they have had a chance to experience and discuss the materials, they can try grouping them. "Which ones are soft/hard/smooth/rough?" and so on.

"Have we all grouped them in the same way?" They could go on to group by using more than one property – for example, hard and rough, or smooth and cold. Do they need to return to the materials to add to their ideas?

Annotated drawing

They could draw pictures to show the materials and then, with or without support, add words to describe the material.

How much more can they do after they have had another go at feeling the materials, classified them or gone on the imaginary journey?

Sequencing

Children could build sequences of materials such as from hard to soft, smooth to rough and so on. Some may need your support to do this.

FEET FAMILY

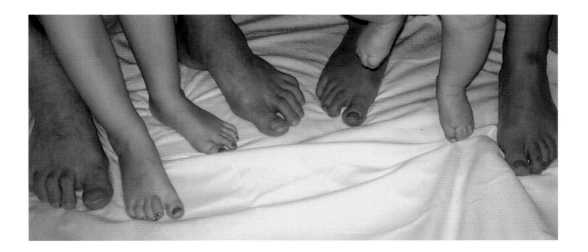

26

What it is

Here the children begin to develop an idea of size variation in humans. They see how much feet vary from one person to the next. Children start by looking at feet in their own class, and get an idea of the range of shapes and sizes. They extend this to other children in the school and into their own families.

They can compare their feet with other animals to look at variation across species (see Extending the activity).

Getting started

- ☐ Collect a few colours of water-based paint.
- ☐ Half-fill some bowls of water, and get some sponges and paper towels for cleaning and drying feet.
- ☐ Collect some large sheets of paper, such as flip chart paper or old rolls of wallpaper. Also collect some sheets of sugar paper.
- ☐ Find some scissors.

 It is a good idea to get children to wash their feet before and after this activity. Avoid sharing towels.

How to use it

Collect footprints from your class. The children can cover the bottom of one foot in paint and step onto paper, or draw around their foot on sugar paper. The footprints can be cut out. Compare their feet, from the smallest to the largest. Discuss whether there would be much difference if they compared their feet with those in other classes.

Get samples from other children. What do your class think will be the difference between their feet and the feet of younger and older children?

If possible, let them take this idea home. They can collect a range of footprints, from baby up to grandma and grandpa. Create sequences of feet, youngest to oldest person or biggest to smallest. What do they notice? They may be surprised that the oldest person is not necessarily the one with the largest feet.

The last time I did this, one child extended the meaning of 'family' to include the cat, the dog and the budgie! It was such a rich resource that it led to the development of the extension activities in this section.

Key questions

What's the difference between the smallest and biggest feet in our class?

Are these children the youngest and the oldest?

Who do you think will have the biggest feet in your family?

Will all the children in the next class have bigger feet than yours?

Do you think the oldest people will have the biggest feet? How will we find out?

Looking for evidence of thinking and learning

In this activity children will have the opportunity to:

- ✓ learn about variation between humans and other animals
- ✓ use and explore the meaning of key vocabulary – humans, animals, feet, paws, claws, smallest, largest, shape, size, similar, different, variation, compare, lifestyle, survive
- ✓ collect data, look for patterns, draw conclusions
- ✓ use visible characteristics to put things in groups.

They can do this by:

- ✓ making a record of their feet
- ✓ collecting footprints from family, friends and people in other classes
- ✓ comparing and contrasting feet
- ✓ grouping feet and looking for connections with the animals' lifestyles
- ✓ identifying the odd one out in a group of animals' feet.

You should see evidence of their thinking and learning in:

- ✓ how they respond to questions
- ✓ the language that they use to describe, compare and contrast
- ✓ how they explain differences in size or shape of different feet
- ✓ how they spot and explain the odd one out
- ✓ their completed class or individual compare and contrast graphic organisers
- ✓ how well they engage in the activities
- ✓ how much they can do without help.

"My feet are bigger than your feet!"

"I've got a toenail on every toe. The one on my little toe is teeny tiny!"

"We've got ten toes altogether!"

Extending the activity

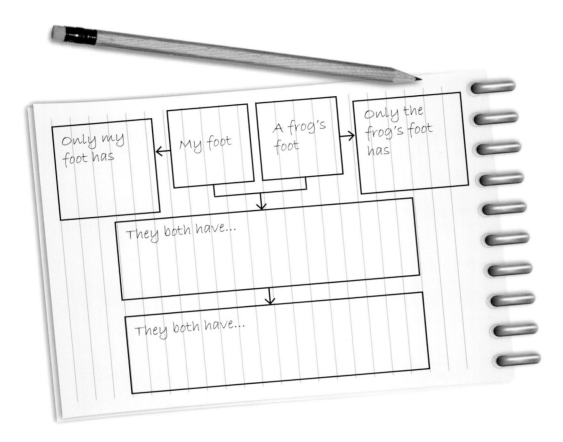

Within the graphic organiser:
- Only my foot has
- My foot
- A frog's foot
- Only the frog's foot has
- They both have...
- They both have...

Children could do a simple Compare and contrast exercise by looking at their own feet and those of older and younger people. They could also compare their feet with the feet of another animal, or compare animals with each other, by using a simple graphic organiser like the one above.

STRATEGY:
Compare and contrast

"Is it only people that have two feet? How many different animals have four feet? Do any have six or eight feet? What about more than eight feet? I wonder how many feet a centipede has? Or a millipede?" Are there questions still to answer? Would looking in books or on the internet help to extend their ideas?

Extending the activity cont.

Classifying and grouping

Children could group the feet of different animals, including humans, by size, number of feet, number of toes, position of toes, presence of scales or feathers or claws, and so on.

Looking at the size and shape of the feet of animals is a good opportunity to discuss their lifestyles. Some of connections between the size and shape of the feet and the animal's lifestyle will be obvious.

"I wonder why we don't have claws or webbed feet?"
"I wonder why the budgie (or the parrot) has claws that curve around?"
"I wonder why the goldfish doesn't have any feet at all?"

Are all the connections obvious? Would looking in books or on the internet help to extend their ideas?

Odd one out

The odd one out strategy enables children to use their knowledge to look for the feet of animals that are different from the rest of the group. Usually there will be more than one possible odd one out, depending on which criteria you use. The children will need to explain why they made their choice of the odd one in the group.

Looking at the photographs of a family of human feet, can they spot the odd one out? For example "This pair is much smaller than the others." or "That one has three toes the same length".

If they were looking at human, horse, rabbit, chicken, frog, they might say:
- the chicken is the only one with feathered legs
- the frog has webbed feet
- the horse is the only one with hooves
- and so on.

Are there any children who are uncertain about the differences? Would looking more carefully at videos, or at pictures, in books or on the internet, help them to make comparisons?

Resources

Suppliers

Millgate House Education Ltd - www.millgatehouse.co.uk:
Science Questions Books
Active Assessment
Benny and other puppets

Instant Snow, Swellgel, large plastic test tubes and digital computer microscopes are available from suppliers such as Timstar, TTS and YPO:
www.timstar.co.uk
www.tts-group.co.uk
www.ypo.co.uk

References

Bird, S. and Saunders, L. (2007) *Rational Food*. Sandbach: Millgate House Publishers.

Naylor, S., Keogh, B. and Goldsworthy, A. (2004) *Active Assessment: thinking, learning and assessment in science*. Sandbach: Millgate House Publishers.

Naylor, B. and Naylor, S. (2000) *Science Questions books*. London: Hodder Children's Books (available through Millgate House Publishers).

Novak, J.D. and Gowin, D.B. (1984) *Learning how to learn*. Cambridge: Cambridge University Press.

Rosen, M. and Oxenbury, H. (1993) *We're going on a bear hunt*. London: Walker Books.

White, R. and Gunstone, R. (1992) *Probing understanding*. London: Falmer Press.

DCELLS Welsh Assembly Government (formerly ACCAC), (2006), Thinking Skills and Assessment for Learning Development Programme: *'Why develop thinking skills and assessment for learning in the classroom?'* and *'How to develop thinking skills and assessment for learning in the classroom'* (released on website).

 **Recipes**

Ice cream

To make a small portion of ice cream

Put a beaker of milk, a spoonful of sugar and some flavouring (Nesquik works well) into a bowl and mix well.
Pour this into a small plastic bag.
Remove as much air as possible and seal it very well.
Put the bag inside another bag and seal it tightly over the first bag.
Fill a small mixing bowl with ice.
Sprinkle on a couple of large tablespoonfuls of salt and a small amount of water so that the ice can move around.
Drop the bag of milk mixture in the ice and shake or stir for five mins.
Remove the bag and you should have ice cream!

Search videojug or other websites for a demo.

Playdough

2 cups of plain flour
2 cups of water
1 cup of salt
2tbs of vegetable oil
2tbs of cream of tartar

Put all ingredients in a pan and stir over a low heat.
Keep stirring until the dough clumps into a ball.
Knead the dough and split into smaller balls.
Add food colouring, if required, and blend in by kneading some more.
You have playdough!

Search videojug or other websites for a demo.

Gloop

Mix 2 cups of cornflour, 1 cup of water, 1 or 2 drops of green food colouring in a bowl.

There's your gloop!

Slime

Put 1/2 cup of water and 1 cup of white (PVA) glue into a bowl.
Stir in 4 drops food colouring if desired.
In another bowl, dissolve 1/2 teaspoon of borax in 1/2 cup of water.
Slowly add the dissolved borax mixture to the glue mixture.
Stir well and there is the slime!